The impact of the Great Famine on Sir William Palmer's estates in Mayo, 1840–69

Maynooth Studies in Local History

SERIES EDITOR Raymond Gillespie

This volume is one of five short books published in the Maynooth Studies in Local History series in 2021. Like their predecessors they range widely over the local experience in the Irish past. Chronologically they range across the 19th century and into the 20th century but they focus on problems that reappeared in almost every period of Irish history. They chronicle the experiences of individuals grappling with their world from the Cork surgeon, Denis Brenan Bullen, in the early 19th century to the politician and GAA administrator Peadar Cowan in the 20th century. From a different perspective they resurrect whole societies under stress from the rural tensions in Knock, Co. Mayo, to the impact of the Famine on Sir William Palmer's estates in Mayo. A rather different sort of institution under stress, Dublin's cattle market, provides the framework for charting the final years of the world that depended on that institution. Geographically they range across the length of the country from Dublin to Cork and westwards into Mayo. Socially they move from those living on the margins of society in Knock through to the prosperous world of the social elite in Cork. In doing so they reveal diverse and complicated societies that created the local past and present the range of possibilities open to anyone interested in studying that past. Those possibilities involve the dissection of the local experience in the complex and contested social worlds of which it is part as people strove to preserve and enhance their positions within their local societies. It also reveals the forces that made for cohesion in local communities and those that drove people apart, whether through large scale rebellion or through acts of inter-personal violence. Such studies of local worlds over such long periods are vital for the future since they not only stretch the historical imagination but provide a longer perspective on the evolution of society in Ireland and help us to understand more fully the complex evolution of the Irish experience. These works do not simply chronicle events relating to an area within administrative or geographically determined boundaries, but open the possibility of understanding how and why particular regions had their own personality in the past. Such an exercise is clearly one of the most exciting challenges for the future and demonstrates the vitality of the study of local history in Ireland.

Like their predecessors, these five short books are reconstructions of the socially diverse worlds of the poor as well as the rich, women as well as men, the geographical marginal of Mayo as well as those located near the centre of power. They reconstruct the way in which those who inhabited those worlds lived their daily lives, often little affected by the large themes that dominate the writing of national history. In addressing these issues, studies such as those presented in these short books, together with their predecessors, are at the forefront of Irish historical research and represent some of the most innovative and exciting work being undertaken in Irish history today. They also provide models that others can follow up and adapt in their own studies of the Irish past. In such ways will we understand better the regional diversity of Ireland and the social and cultural basis for that diversity. They, with their predecessors, convey the vibrancy and excitement of the world of Irish local history today.

Maynooth Studies in Local History: Number 149

The impact of the Great Famine on Sir William Palmer's estates in Mayo, 1840–69

David Byrne

FOUR COURTS PRESS

Set in 10pt on 12pt Bembo by
Carrigboy Typesetting Services for
FOUR COURTS PRESS LTD
7 Malpas Street, Dublin 8, Ireland
www.fourcourtspress.ie
and in North America for
FOUR COURTS PRESS
c/o IPG, 814 N Franklin St, Chicago, IL 60610

ISBN 978–1–84682–973–4

Printed in Ireland
by SprintPrint, Dublin.

Contents

Acknowledgments

I wish to acknowledge the help given to me in the completion of this work by many people. I am very grateful to the staff of NUI Maynooth Library, the National Library of Ireland, the National Archives of Ireland, the Irish Architectural Archive and Mary Higgins in TCD Library. I owe a special word of thanks to my fellow classmates for their help and encouragement over the last two years and to Dr Gerard Moran and Dr Brian Dornan for their suggestions and assistance. I wish to express my gratitude to Mr Roger Graham-Palmer for his interest in my work. In particular I would like to thank my supervisor Professor Raymond Gillespie for his patience, advice and incisive analysis which has greatly helped me with my work. Finally, I owe great debt to my wife Mary and my children Kevin and Laura who made many sacrifices to enable me finish my work.

The author, David Byrne, died in 2019 prior to the publication of this book. His wife Mary and children Kevin and Laura would like to thank Dr Gerard Moran for updating the text, Anthony Doyle for his help in bringing David's work through to publication, Colum O'Riordan of the Irish Architectural Archive for his help with the image of Kenure Park and Mr Archie Graham-Palmer for the images of Cefn Park, Wrexham, and of Sir William Henry Roger Palmer.

Introduction

This book aims to examine the impact of the Great Famine on the estate of the Palmer family, situated in Mayo. To do this, it is necessary to examine the social and economic conditions that prevailed on this estate in the 1830s and early 1840s, the impact of the potato failure on the population, and the gradual normalization of conditions during the 1850s and early 1860s.

Mayo was one of the counties worst affected by the Famine, its population declining by 29 per cent between 1841 and 1851, from 388,887 to 274,499, largely the result of high mortality levels rather than emigration. As a result it has attracted much attention from historians in works such as Cecil Woodham-Smith's *The Great Hunger*,[1] Mary E. Daly's *The Famine in Ireland*,[2] Cormac Ó Gráda's *The Great Irish Famine*,[3] and Christine Kinealy's *This great calamity: the Irish Famine, 1845–52*,[4] which deal with the Famine on a national basis and all draw extensively on evidence for the Famine period from Mayo. Donald E. Jordan's *Land and popular politics in Ireland: County Mayo from the Plantation to the Land War* examines the social, economic and political changes that occurred in Co. Mayo from the Elizabethan plantations to the land war in the early 1880s.[5] However, it is widely acknowledged by historians that there is a dearth of regional studies related to the Famine period in most counties in Ireland. Cormac Ó Gráda in 1995 pointed out the need for academic local studies of the Famine period:

> The lack of Irish research on the famine is well reflected by the paucity of regional studies ... scholarly accounts of the famine at local level are almost non-existent ... much could be learned from local studies about ... the role of landlords.[6]

Prior to 1995, when the sesquicentenary commemoration occurred, little had been written on the Great Famine, the exceptions being Canon John O'Rourke's *The Great Irish Famine*, Woodham-Smith's *The Great Hunger*, Mary Daly's *The Famine in Ireland* and Ó Gráda's *The Great Irish Famine*.[7] Since 1995 a large corpus of work has been published that has increased our understanding of this major event in Irish history. These works include James S. Donnelly's *The Great Irish Potato Famine* and Ciarán Ó Murchadha's *The Great Famine, Ireland's agony, 1845–52*.[8] While these provided an insight into the national situation and at times highlight the catastrophe that took place in places like Skibbereen and west Kerry, they failed to provide an adequate understanding of what happened locally. As local history is an important building block in our understanding of the national situation, it is crucial that we examine how the Great Famine impacted local communities at a parish, estate and county level. Over the last 25 years a number of excellent local studies have been completed to fill this void. These include Ciarán Ó Murchadha's *Sable wings over the land: Ennis, County Clare and its wider community during the Great Famine*; Kathleen Villiers-Tuthill's *Patient endurance: the Great Famine in Connemara* and Bryan MacMahon's *The Great Famine in Tralee and north Kerry*.[9] In addition, more specialized studies on the Famine have been published giving an additional insight into communities such as women and children at both a national and local level. Among these studies are *Women and the Great Hunger* edited by Christine Kinealy, Jason King and Ciarán Reilly, and *Children and the Great Hunger in Ireland* edited by Christine Kinealy, Jason King and Gerard Moran.[10]

In their guide to surviving estate records in Ireland, Ó Gráda and Eiríksson emphasize the necessity for local studies of landed estates during the Famine period:

> At the time of the great famine, most of the land of Ireland was owned by about ten thousand people … landed proprietors were key figures in the economic, social and political life of Ireland before the famine. They wielded enormous power. What they did during the famine, what more they could have done to save lives, and how they were affected by the famine remain controversial issues. Curiously enough, historians have not touched on these topics much.[11]

This book attempts to address some of the issues raised by Ó Gráda and Eiríksson by examining the impact of the Famine on one of Mayo's largest estates and analysing the social, economic and political role of Sir William Palmer during this period. How Lord Palmer managed his estates and what he did or failed to do before, during and after the Famine, are central themes of this book.

The study of the Palmer estates is important as it covers such a long period and highlights the impact that the Great Famine had on the property and its tenants. Comparisons can be made with other properties not only nationally, but also in Mayo and adjoining counties as a number of studies have recently been undertaken such as Michael Kelly's *Struggle and strife on a Mayo estate, 1833–1903: the Nolans of Logboy and their tenants*,[12] and Tom Crehan's *Marcella Gerrard's Galway estate, 1820–70*,[13] which analyse estate management and how landowners dealt with the economic implications of the Famine. The Famine not only had major consequences for tenants, but also for landowners as many were forced to sell all or part of their properties to avoid financial insolvency. Contemporary accounts and recent historical analysis indicate that many did little to alleviate the plight of the poor during this period. While these generalizations treat landed proprietors as a homogenous group there were those who adopted a paternalistic approach towards their tenants, in contrast to others like Palmer, who took a more mercenary stand. Only when more comprehensive studies of individual estates are conducted will a true picture of the relationship between landlord and tenant during this period emerge. This can only take place where the relevant estate records and sources are available.

While landlords often did not reside on their properties their power and authority still extended beyond the walls of their estates because they controlled local and parliamentary politics. They, or their representatives, were involved in local politics as poor law guardians, as members of the grand juries and as magistrates. Those with large estates could influence the parliamentary elections in their constituencies, and some even sat in the House of Lords. While they held such local and national political power, it was often questionable whether they served their own interests or the views and concerns of their constituents. This only changed with the enactment of the Secret Ballot act in 1872 and the extension of the franchise in 1885. Landlords were able to dictate issues and the outcome of elections through threats and intimidation, as was evident on the Palmer estate.

The landlord had a pivotal influence in the social, economic and political affairs of the area and community that he controlled. Many managed their properties with an iron fist, leaving their tenants in no doubt as to their power and authority. Estate rules were in place that could affect every aspect of the tenants' lives: from who they could marry to who they could vote for at election time. The strongest weapon that the landlord possessed and which impacted on the lives of their tenants was the threat of eviction and in a county like Mayo where there were few alternative employment opportunities to agriculture, this was akin to death.

This book begins with an overview of the pre-Famine social and economic structures on the estates. The first chapter sets out to explain the geographical position of the estates, how the Palmer family came to own land in Mayo, the system of land tenure that existed on the estates before the Famine, the social and economic conditions of the poor on the property in the pre-Famine period and how Lord Palmer's absenteeism contributed to the economic difficulties faced by his tenants, in contrast to resident landlords who made significant efforts to alleviate poverty on their properties.

The principal sources used in this chapter are a private valuation survey of the Palmer estates in Mayo carried out in the early 1840s, the alphabetical register of leases belonging to the Palmer Mayo property, the minutes of evidence from the 1830s Poor Inquiry and the minutes of evidence of the Devon Commission. These sources provide a wealth of information about pre-Famine conditions on the Palmer estates and in Mayo in general. However, the valuation survey of the Palmer estates gives no description of houses valued at less than £5 per annum nor the crops grown on tillage land.[14] Similarly, the register of leases of the Palmer property is incomplete. Leases recorded in the register run from number one to number 503, yet there are only 431 entries in this register, so 72 leases were not recorded in the register. Also, some ejectments and surrenders are not dated.[15] These limitations make definite conclusions about ejectments, surrenders and conditions of tenure impossible.

The second chapter attempts to analyse the extent to which pre-Famine structures contributed to the distress on the Palmer estates. It sets out to describe Famine conditions on the Palmer property in the context of other regions in Mayo, and attempts to demonstrate how the distress on the Palmer lands was exacerbated by the system of landholding on the estate. The social and economic impact of the Famine on different parts of the property is analysed and this chapter seeks to explain the different rates of population change within the various parts of the Mayo estate as well as between the property generally and the county overall by looking at evictions, surrendering of leases and emigration.

The principal sources used in the second chapter are local newspapers, particularly the *Tirawley Herald*, the register of leases of the Palmer estates, Islandeady and Aughavel parish registers, incoming letters of the Famine Relief Commission and a wide range of parliamentary papers such as correspondence relating to the relief of distress, eviction returns and the 1851 census. Again, these sources though valuable in helping to build up a picture of Famine conditions in Mayo, also present problems. For instance, it is not specified in the eviction returns if the numbers listed as evicted pertain to individuals or families so it is difficult to accurately quantify the number of evictions from an estate or a region.[16] It is estimated that between 250,000 and 500,000 were evicted in the country during and in the immediate years after the Famine.[17] Similarly, the parish registers are incomplete in some cases, making time-series comparisons difficult.

The third chapter examines the social and economic conditions on Palmer's Mayo estates in the aftermath of the Famine by looking at the political role of Lord Palmer, post-Famine evictions, the system of land tenure after the Famine, the continued demographic decline and the recovery in the agricultural sector and in rentals.

The main sources used for the post-famine era are the George Henry Moore papers, the 1863 rent book of the Palmer Mayo estates, and a range of official sources such as the Primary Valuation of Tenements, the 1861 census and agricultural statistics from 1847 and 1856. The Primary Valuation of Tenements[18] only lists immediate lessors so the level of subletting on the Palmer estates during the 1850s is difficult to estimate exactly.

1. Conditions on the Palmer estates in the pre-Famine period

After the death of his father on 29 May 1840, Sir William Henry Roger Palmer (commonly called Sir Roger Palmer), then aged 37, inherited a vast estate with lands in Ireland, Wales and England. The principal family residences were Kenure Park, a large elaborately furnished late Georgian house in Dublin (fig. 2) and Cefn Park in Wrexham (fig. 3). In total, the Palmer estates exceeded 100,000 acres and the greatest portion of this – over 80,000 acres – were situated in Co. Mayo.[1]

1. Sir William Henry Roger Palmer, fourth baronet
(Courtesy of Roger Graham-Palmer and Archie Graham-Palmer)

2. Kenure Park, the Dublin home of Sir William Henry Roger Palmer[2]
(Courtesy of the Irish Architectural Archive)

3. Cefn Park, the Wrexham home of Sir William Henry Roger Palmer
(Courtesy of Roger Graham-Palmer and Archie Graham-Palmer)

The Palmer property in Mayo was not geographically contiguous but was in fact dispersed throughout the county and was situated in five baronies namely Tirawley in the north of the county, Burrishoole in the west, Gallen in the east and Carra and Murrisk in the south (fig. 4).[3] Land quality on the property varied from region to region and within individual townlands, with tracts of fertile agricultural land, often alongside rivers, and large tracts of blanket bog. The total recorded population of the estate was 22,797 in 1841.[4] In both physical and demographic terms, the Tirawley portion of the property was the largest, containing 50,841 acres in the 1840s[5] and 45 per cent of the estate population in 1841.

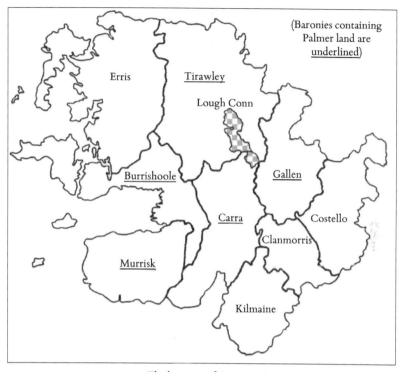

(Baronies containing Palmer land are underlined)

Erris

Tirawley

Lough Conn

Burrishoole

Gallen

Carra

Costello

Clanmorris

Murrisk

Kilmaine

4. The baronies of Co. Mayo[6]

The Palmer family had a long history of involvement in Ireland. The first known transaction of land involving a member of the Palmer family was a lease by Sir Arthur Gore of Castlegore, Co. Mayo, of the village and lands of Boghadone, a townland south of Crossmolina, dated 28 June 1671, to Roger Palmer of Farra, Co. Mayo.[7] In November 1684, Roger Palmer of Palmerstown, Co. Mayo, received a grant of large estates in Co. Mayo from King Charles II and thereafter, through a series of purchases, grants and judiciously arranged marriages, the property was enlarged and consolidated.

Upon his succession, Sir William Henry Roger Palmer became the fourth baronet of Castle Lacken, a title that had been created by patent for his grandfather in 1777. He took immediate steps to confirm his new status and to manage his estates. He was elected to membership of the Carlton Club in London on 2 May 1841.[8] Carlton Club membership was taken out by members of the Conservative party, the party of the vast majority of Ireland's landed gentry, so Sir William's political affiliations can be identified by this action. Also in 1841, Sir William applied to the chief herald of Ireland for a grant and confirmation of Arms that he and his family could then legally use and bear.[9] He also commissioned a private valuation survey of his entire Mayo and Sligo estates to help determine the value of his property and the letting value it would generate. Each townland on the estate was measured and mapped, and soil quality was analysed, making administration of the vast property more manageable.[10]

This private valuation survey gives an insight into the system of land tenure on many of the townlands of the Palmer Mayo estates as does the register of leases of the Palmer Mayo properties.[11] This was a complex system, with local gentry, large farmers, small farmers and a large population of labourers and destitute poor. Leaseholders held denominations as small as an acre or less, particularly in urban regions such as around Crossmolina, while others leased extensive properties. William Byrne, for instance, held a lease for three lives on land in the townland of Keenaghbeg that extended for 1,084 acres.[12] Leases were held by individuals and by groups of tenants who obtained leases in common.[13] Out of a total of 431 recorded leases, 99 or 23 per cent of leases were held jointly or in common. Lands adjoining urban areas were more likely to be held by leaseholders. For instances, the townland of Cartron Gilbert that adjoins Crossmolina is named in a total of 21 leases spanning the period 1816–59, while Crossmolina townland is named in 16 leases between 1809 and 1881. Conversely, rural townlands, especially those with extensive tracts of marginal lands, were less likely to be leased. In Moneyneirin and Derry Upper for example, both situated in bogland to the south of Crossmolina, only one lease was recorded as being issued in each case for the period 1718–1884 while the nearby townlands of Mungaun (population 34 in 1841) and Ballyknock (population 272 in 1841)[14] have no leases recorded for the same period.[15] Therefore, only a very small proportion of tenants actually held leases and most were tenants-at-will.

On several townlands there were resident gentry or middlemen who were leasing land and houses from the Palmer estate. The parish of Lacken for instance contained ten townlands belonging to the Palmer properties. This parish was surveyed as part of the estate survey between June and July 1841. Houses valued at £5 per annum or over were described by the surveyor. Carrowmore townland contained Carrowmore House, valued at £22 per annum, and was rented by Roger Palmer. The townland of Castlelackan Demesne containing the large house of Castlelackan was leased to Edward Knox and valued at £58 per annum.[16] However, residence in a big house was confined to a privileged few. The majority of the townlands in this parish and elsewhere on the Palmer estate contained no £5 houses. Instead they contained the dwellings of the ordinary smallholders and labourers, property that was not commented on by the surveyors. In Co. Mayo in general, most of the agricultural holdings were small in size in the 1840s. Out of a total of 53,003 holdings in the county in 1847, 68 per cent were less than 15 acres in size while only 13 per cent of holdings exceeded 30 acres.[17]

The Mayo estates Sir William inherited while extensive were, for the most part, occupied by impoverished people who faced a constant struggle to provide themselves with food and to pay the rent. The social and economic conditions of the vast majority of the tenants on the Palmer property in 1840 could hardly have been much worse. Unemployment and underemployment were commonplace, living conditions were appalling, diet was poor and in general most people lived in conditions of abject poverty, enduring a constant struggle to pay rents and to provide the basic human necessities of food, clothing and shelter.

The first *Report of the Commissioners for Inquiring into the Conditions of the poorer classes in Ireland*, published 1835–6, gives a valuable insight into conditions on the Palmer estate and elsewhere in Mayo in the period just before Sir William's succession. Evidence relating to the parish of Aughagower was provided by the Revd Peter Ward, PP. This parish, in the barony of Burrishoole, contained two townlands belonging to the Palmer estates. Houses in this parish were described as being:

> Mostly built of stone, sometimes with and sometimes without mortar ... the furniture consists of one or two bedsteads, one or two stools and two small tables ... one half of the people sleep on the floor on straw; and about a seventh part of them scarcely have any blankets, covered only by the tattered clothes they wear. I know many families, sometimes eight in number, without a single blanket.[18]

Evidence for the parish of Islandeady, situated in the baronies of Burrishoole and Carra, was provided by Theobald Burke, JP. This parish contained 40 townlands belonging to the Palmer estates. Cabins here were described as 'built of loose stones, sometimes dashed; their furniture consists of two or three chairs, and a large form, upon which they eat. Their bedding [is] very bad'.[19] In the parish of Killasser, situated in the barony of Gallen, where four townlands belonging to the Palmer property were located, the Revd J. McNulty, PP, described cabins as:

> generally built along the verges of bogs, sometimes dug into a turf bank, and covered with heath or rushes, sometimes built with sods. No bedsteads in many instances; no bed to lie on; but a wad of straw or heath, with very little bed clothes.[20]

William Ormsby, an agent of Lord Palmer, giving evidence for the parish of Crossmolina, which contained 40 townlands belonging to the Palmer estates, described the cabins of the poor as 'mostly wretched, scarcely any furniture except a bed and dresser'.[21] Similar evidence about dwellings is recorded for other parts of the property.

These witnesses also generally agreed that for a variety of reasons, living conditions, if anything, were getting worse rather than better. This deterioration was variously attributed to the collapse in agricultural prices after the Napoleonic wars ended, the collapse of the local linen industry in certain areas and high rents and low farm output. However, the most frequent reason cited for the decline in living standards among the poorer classes of Mayo was the rapid population growth and the subdivision of holdings which this engendered. Theobald Burke, in his evidence to the Commissioners regarding the parish of Islandeady, declared:

> The condition of the poor during the war was prosperous in the extreme; since then their condition has deteriorated considerably; the population is, notwithstanding, increasing to a vast extent. I regret to say that to the habit of subdividing their holdings with their grown families I attribute the principal cause of the poverty.[22]

The main work that the poor of the Palmer estates could expect was that as agricultural labourers. Very few had constant sustainable employment. Periods of work were related to the agricultural cycle so employment was seasonal, mainly in spring and autumn. Most agricultural labourers were seasonally unemployed in the summer and winter. Some labourers in Mayo were able to obtain task work – doing odd jobs for the local gentry – and this enabled them to earn their rents rather than having to pay them in cash. However, on the estates of the major landowners in the county, such as the Palmer and Lucan properties, the landlords were absentees and tenants generally did not have this option.

The seasonal nature of the agricultural employment and the low level of income that resulted, led to many labourers migrating to Britain on a seasonal basis from the Palmer estates during this period. This migration was facilitated by the advent of a regular and inexpensive steamboat service between Ireland and Britain after 1816. Steam transport removed the last obstacle that deterred many peasants from migrating, namely the difficulty and expense of a sea voyage.[23] Theobald Burke, in his evidence before the Poor Law Commission about the parish of Islandeady, told the commissioners 'I suppose that at least 100 leave this parish every year to go to England during the harvest; they return usually in September or October'.[24] The Revd John McNulty, giving evidence about migrant labourers from Killasser, said: 'Two-thirds I should suppose or one half at least, of the men in the parish go to England for two to three months every season, to obtain employment'.[25] The Revd M. Conway, PP, providing evidence about the parishes of Kilfian and Rathrea, barony of Tirawley, on which there were 11 townlands from the Palmer estates, declared: 'sixty-one have left the parish this year; twenty-five of them to England. Several were prepared to go, only for the speedy return of some who had a bad account of it, having pawned their clothes'.[26]

Earnings from this seasonal migration were a vital source of income to many Mayo families. Harvest wages in Ireland never equalled those in England and the seasonal migrant often earned about £5 to bring back to Ireland although the sum varied with the district and the weather.[27] Co. Mayo had the highest rate of seasonal migration of any county during the 1830s with 37 migrants per 1,000 of the population annually compared with 21 per 1,000 in Roscommon and 18 per 1,000 in Leitrim.[28] Many of these seasonal migrants from Mayo lived on the Palmer estates and depended for their living on the seasonal earnings from England. Between one-half and two-thirds of all the men in the parish of Killaser (which contained four townlands belonging to the Palmer property) went to England for a period each year while in Toomore (which contained three townlands from the Palmer estate) there were two migratory labourers for every five families.[29]

Many of these seasonal migrants were married men forced to leave their families behind while they migrated. This caused intense hardship for these families who were often forced to depend on their impoverished neighbours for food and shelter. Begging was often forced upon these families as the only means of survival. William Ormsby's evidence about the parish of Crossmolina states: 'married men often leave their wives to subsist by charity (or begging) during their absence'.[30] The Revd B. Burke, PP, gave evidence about the parish of Oughavale in the barony of Murrisk which contained ten townlands from the Palmer estates. In relation to these seasonal migrants he states: 'Some are married men. Their wives and children subsist on the potatoes they raised on their little farms or con-acres ... and those who have no potatoes beg through the country'.[31] Various witnesses also pointed out that the local community in each parish were sympathetic to the plight of these families forced to beg and many people, despite their own poverty, gave free lodgings to beggars.

The diet of the poorer labourers was almost exclusively of potatoes and milk, which on rare occasions was supplemented with fish, meat or even seaweed. Rapid population growth in Mayo combined with subdivision of farms into smaller units meant that people needed a potato crop that produced a high yield from a small amount of (often infertile) land. Potatoes called lumpers were grown and these were generally regarded by witnesses to the Poor Law Commission to be poor in quality and nourishment. The condition of clothing was also very poor. Revd Ward of Aughagower stated:

> There are not in this parish twenty men who have at this time two pairs of good shoes ... one-third of them cannot come to mass on the Lord's day for want of clothing; and as for the females, their condition is still worse, there are not thirty in the entire parish ... who wear shoes constantly throughout the year.[32]

These descriptions from a large number of witnesses about the conditions of the poorer classes in Mayo in the 1830s provide us with a vivid insight into the social and economic conditions prevailing on the Palmer estates when Sir William succeeded his father in 1840.

Sir William Palmer, like many of his contemporaries, chose not to live in Mayo. His principal residences were in Kenure Park in Dublin and Cefn Park in Wrexham and he did not maintain a demesne in Mayo. Kenure Park in Rush, Co. Dublin, was a large late Georgian house with an elaborate front portico designed by George Papworth, the noted architect. In contrast with the cabins of his Mayo tenants, this three-storeyed house consisted of a large entrance hall, dining rooms, offices and 14 bedrooms on the top floor. The house was elaborately furnished with chippendale and chinese pieces and contained an extensive collection of paintings and portraits. The gardens around the demesne extended for over 200 acres. Sir William spent over £10,000 in renovations to the house during the 1850s.[33]

Landlords who resided on their estates were generally in close touch with their tenants and could see for themselves the life conditions of their people. Absentees on the other hand often had little or no knowledge of the real needs of their tenants. The agents who ran the estates of absentee landlords often placed greater emphasis upon money than upon life and their priority was the collection of rents rather than a contented tenantry.[34] This often resulted in 'feelings of mistrust and antipathy between owners and occupiers which … eliminated any possibility of benevolence on the one hand or of loyalty on the other'.[35] As such, absenteeism from Mayo and residence in elaborate mansions formed a gulf between Lord Palmer and his tenants and enabled Lord Palmer to detach himself both physically and mentally from the vast majority of the occupiers of his Mayo properties.

As an absentee landlord, the management of his estates in Mayo was handed over to agents and middlemen, and the tenants lost out on considerable local economic benefits that a landlord's demesne engendered. These benefits usually entailed payments to labourers and others for carrying out necessary ongoing tasks associated with the running of a demesne property. At Kenure Park, between 25 and 35 people were employed by the estate depending on the time of year. Accounts for the period 1870–2, although later than the period under discussion, help to illustrate the impact of Palmer's demesne on the local economy. These accounts show that total weekly wages varied from £10 to £29 to the work force who were classified as garden men, farm men, demesne men, house men and keepers. This local labour force were paid an average wage of 1s. 6d. per day for a six-day week and carried out a variety of tasks such as ploughing, repair work, plastering, fixing walls and turning manure.[36] These wages contrasted favourably with labourers wages in Mayo where earnings varied from as little as 5½d. per day to 1s. per day in the 1840s and work was often short term and irregular.[37] Similarly, on the Clanmorris estate in south Mayo, an account of miscellaneous disbursements was kept to record payments to locals for services rendered. Among the entries recorded in this account in 1867 were:

June 18   Cash paid to M McNulty 7 days carting stones and repairing roads
               at Mayo 15 shillings.
July 9   Paid John Griffin for stones for new house for shepherds at
               Ballymalavil £1.00.
August 8   Paid Pat Hughes surveying con-acre turf of 1867 £4 8s. 3d.
September 6   Paid D Bridgman for tuition £127 10s.
October 2   Paid Michael Lally labour at Learmount £4.00
               Paid Pat and W Preudey drawing stones and building herd house at
               Ballymalavil, roofing it and making doors and windows £12 10s.
December 12   Paid Robert Neill shoemaker 12s.
December 13   Paid John McNulty, Butcher 5s.[38]

These accounts illustrate the local economic benefits to the community that resulted from the presence of a landlord's demesne. The tenants on Palmer's Mayo estates were economically disadvantaged by their landlord's decision to reside outside the county.

In the early 1840s with the population growing rapidly and the subdivision of farms into ever-decreasing holdings commonplace, economic conditions in Mayo were steadily dis-improving. Several members of the local gentry took steps to improve their properties and to increase the welfare of their tenants. In his evidence to the Devon Commission, George V. Jackson, a local land proprietor who lived at Carrowmore, near Ballina, outlined the improvements he had made to his estate by breaking up rundale settlements to create individual allotments, a process called striping. Referring to a townland on his property he declared:

> I found it without roads, without drains, held in common … by twenty
> occupants; the houses all clustered together, and very wretched. I made
> roads through it and made drains. I had it subdivided into allotments,
> giving each person as much as I could, and placed each man on his own
> allotment, and the result has been, that they have brought every little spot
> of it into cultivation. Parts which were lying waste for fifty years are now
> producing crops, and the whole district is very much improved, and the
> tenantry greatly improved in their condition.[39]

He also gave details about how he had financed improvements on his estate and allowed his tenants the benefit of any improvements which they themselves had made. Significantly, Jackson believed that tenants of the properties of resident proprietors fared better than those whose landlords who were absent stating 'I think where the proprietor can attend himself to everything that goes on, the tenantry are much better off than on those estates which are differently circumstanced.'[40]

George Irwin, a land agent from Greenalue, near Ballina, agreed with the opinion about absenteeism expressed by George Jackson. In his evidence to the commissioners, about the difference between the estates of resident and non-resident proprietors, Irwin stated 'There may be from forty to fifty men employed in common labour alone, by the resident proprietor, the absentee does nothing.'[41]

Unlike some of the local proprietors, Sir William Palmer was not an improving landlord. He gave little encouragement to his tenantry to improve their holdings. William Bland, a tenant of Sir Richard O'Donnell and Lord Sligo, lived adjacent to 500 acres of the Palmer estate near Westport. In his evidence to the commissioners, he stated:

> Lord Sligo gives some assistance amounting to 2*d*. a perch, for drains, where the drains executed would come to at least 5*d*., so the tenant pays 3*d*. He pays half of all the main drains, and so does Sir Richard O'Donnell. Sir Roger Palmer gives no encouragement of the kind, nor does Mr Knox of Castlerea.[42]

Fredrick Cavendish of Castlebar, proprietor and editor of the *Castlebar Telegraph* newspaper, gave evidence to the commissioners about distraining and evictions on the Lucan, Sligo and Palmer estates. When asked about the methods used to recover rent from defaulting tenants he stated:

> If there is no distress on the land, they go by process; if there is any distress on the land they seize; and after seizure, if any balance is due, they process for the rest.[43]

When asked about the prevalence of middlemen and the profits they made he stated:

> There are two or three estates held by middlemen ... for instance, a nephew of mine, Lord Kilmaine, has two estates in this neighbourhood, and a great number of the persons on those estates derive more profit from them than he does; and so on Sir Roger Palmer's estates.[44]

Cavendish believed that tenants renting land from middlemen where the landed proprietor was absent were disadvantaged and exploited, and that middlemen rather than the absentee landlord were the main beneficiaries of the estate rentals:

> the landlord derives very little advantage from the letting of the land to the middleman. The middlemen derive not only considerable profit, but, under the terms of their agreements with their tenants, they get labour and duty work done ... the people are obliged to neglect their own tillage and give it to the middleman. That prevails to a considerable extent upon

Lord Kilmaine's and Sir Roger Palmer's estates. If Sir Roger Palmer's estate was out of lease, it would produce £60,000 a year. Several parties under him have a profit of £1,000 a year.[45]

The body of evidence, collected in 1844, outlines the difficulties faced by landlords and tenants on the eve of the Famine in Mayo. On the estates of the large absentee landed proprietors such as the Palmer estate, tenants often had to contend with additional problems. They were out of sight of their landlord, exploited by middlemen, given little encouragement to improve their holdings by the landowner and lost out on the employment and economic opportunities afforded to those whose landlord was resident. They also frequently had to contend with distraining or eviction when rents were overdue. These factors were to prove catastrophic for the tenants of the Palmer estates when the potato crop failed and Famine conditions broke out the following year.

2. The impact of the Great Famine on the Palmer Mayo estates

The potato crop in Ireland had a history of failure during the early 19th century. In 1816 a serious failure occurred. In 1821 and 1822 the potato crop failed completely in Munster and Connacht. In 1831 and 1832 the crop failed in Mayo, Galway and Donegal and in 1836 and 1837 extensive failures were recorded throughout Ireland.[1] Serious distress afflicted Mayo in 1816, 1822, 1831, 1832 and 1836 following these failures.[2] For instance, the *Castlebar Telegraph* reported in 1831 that several areas of Mayo were experiencing severe difficulties:

> [In Achill] ... 3,000 persons to be in want of the necessaries of life, several of whom, are expiring from inability to obtain food – the population are existing like the birds of the air, on what they can gather from the fields, and a scanty supply of shellfish and weeds ... in the district of Newport twelve people have died of starvation ... The accounts from Crossmolina, Killala, Ballina and several parishes in Tyrawly ... convey a lamentable picture of human misery which is hourly increasing ... thousands will perish unless prompt relief is procured.[3]

Regular potato crop failures in the decades preceding the 1840s meant therefore that the failure in 1845 was neither new nor unexpected.

The first reports of impending disaster were published in Mayo in September 1845. Tirawley, where Lord Palmer owned 50,841 acres, was densely populated and contained a large proportion of people who depended upon the potato crop for subsistence. In its edition dated 18 September 1845 the *Tyrawley Herald* carried reports of potato blight in England but pointed out that there was no blight locally.[4] However, by 23 October 1845, the *Herald* editorial was calling on landlords to be 'compassionate and help tenants who must endure the utmost privation because of the dreaded crop failure'.[5]

The re-appearance of the blight by June 1846 led to widespread distress in Mayo during the severe winter of 1846–7. A letter addressed to the central relief committee of the Society of Friends dated 29 December 1846 described conditions in Crossmolina parish at that time. This parish contained 40 townlands belonging to the Palmer estate. This letter stated:

> This parish contains 20,000 inhabitants, one half of whom are in a state of destitution. The village of Crossmolina contains 2,000 inhabitants, one

half of whom are in a state of desperate want. This population is made up of farmers dispossessed of their farms throughout the country, who were too poor to go to America and are obliged to remain depending on a casual day's labour.[6]

In the nearby parish of Kilfian where five townlands from the Palmer property were located, the correspondent painted an equally bleak picture:

The wretched condition of this parish, containing a dense population of pauper tenantry, is truly deplorable ... few would believe the sad and sickening account ... the poor are without money, food, clothing or hope of relief. No less than eight deaths have occurred from want of food within the last week ... and dysentery prevails to a fearful extent.[7]

Lord Palmer also held extensive estates around the Killala district in northern Tirawley. In its issue dated 14 January 1847 the *Tyrawley Herald* carried a letter from James Collins, dean of Killala, which stated:

The distress in this neighbourhood has for some months past, been quite appalling and it increases in fearful magnitude every day ... Crowds of starving creatures are round my house almost every moment of the day... The rural district around my house is large and populous but totally devoid of landed gentry. The landlords are absentees, and unable to give aid to any extent, because of incumbrances, and non-payment of their rents.[8]

Mervyn Pratt, in a letter to the Society of Friends Famine relief commission about conditions in Crossmolina, also distinguished between resident and absentee landlords in their response to the suffering of their tenants:

We have found no easy matter the few resident gentlemen with scarcely an exception, having not only spent as much of their means as they can afford in endeavouring to alleviate the heart rending sufferings of their own wretched tenantry as well as the still greater sufferings of the (tenants of) the heartless absentees who with a solitary exception up to this ... have not given the slightest assistance.[9]

These accounts illustrate the conditions of distress faced by Palmer's tenants. They attribute a significant part of the cause of their distress to the fact that their landlord did not live in the district, a point emphasized by Colonel Jackson, a resident landlord who wrote in September 1847:

We are consumed by the hives of human beings that exist on the properties of the absentees. On my right and my left are proprietors such as I allude to. I am overwhelmed and ruined by them. The proprietors will do nothing. All the burden of relief and employment falls on me.[10]

The resident local gentry did attempt to help the destitute in Co. Mayo and tenants on those estates at least had some efforts to relieve distress made on their behalf. As early as May 1846, the *Tyrawley Herald* carried a report about improvements to the river Moy, commenting:

> too much gratitude cannot be felt towards these gentlemen (Sir R. O'Donnell, Col. Gore, Patrick Crean, George V. Jackson), for their exertions on this and every other occasion in advancing the interests of the country and more particularly ... to alleviate the distress which may follow the failure of the potato crop.[11]

Many of the local gentry also served as poor law guardians, responsible for administering relief and running workhouses in their own poor law unions, administrative units made up of townlands. It is difficult to give a comprehensive assessment of the work of the poor law guardians as there are no known complete surviving sets of minute books for any of the unions in Co. Mayo.[12] In addition, many individuals initiated efforts to help the destitute in whatever way they could. The *Tyrawley Herald* carried numerous reports on events held and contributions made towards Famine relief. For instance, the edition dated 4 March 1847 carried an acknowledgment by Mrs Palmer of Carrowmore, near Killala, of £5 from a Mrs L'Estrange of Gortner Abbey towards the Lackan soup kitchen. In the same edition a report was printed about the work of Owenmore Ladies Relief Society which superintended the distribution of soup and meal.

Sir Richard O'Donnell of Newport wrote to the Famine relief committee on 18 September 1846 with an offer to help with Famine relief work in his own district:

> I regret to have to inform you that in the districts of Newport, Achill and Ballycroy, the very greatest want of food prevails ... I write therefore to request that the government may without delay send provisions ... I shall provide in each locality a store free of expense, or if the government will sell a cargo of meal to me at the present price ... I have no objection to purchase it for the use of the people.[13]

Other local initiatives were also undertaken. For instance, Col. Knox Gore of Beleek Manor outside Ballina approached the Society of Friends early in 1849 for an interest-free loan of £800 to enable him to appropriate 100 acres of waste land and to employ a number of labourers to reclaim it. An interest-free loan was provided for 12 months and was repaid in full, and the Society of Friends declared themselves well satisfied with the experiment.[14] Lord Palmer himself made contributions to some of the organizations concerned with Famine relief in those areas in which he held land. For instance, subscriptions to the Killala parochial relief fund for the distressed poor show that in December 1846, Lord Palmer donated £20 through his agent Thomas Ormsby.[15] Similarly, subscriptions to the Crossmolina soup kitchen included a donation of £50 from Lord Palmer.[16] However, despite this work, the conditions of the poor continued to deteriorate in north Mayo in the late 1840s. Commenting on the distress and the decision to drop the public works the *Tyrawley Herald* reported in November 1847:

> The people of Tyrawley are in a most awful condition of distress. Many of them are as badly situated as they were at the worst period of the past year, whilst no small proportion of them are even worse off in circumstances than they were twelve months ago. Then they had the means of obtaining some small degree of subsistence as they were employed at the public works. Now they have no employment nor food of any description.[17]

The burden of Famine relief was transferred to the board of guardians in the various poor law unions. These guardians sought to finance their relief efforts through the collection of rates, and landlords were obliged to pay rates for their tenants with a rateable valuation of £4 or less. Many landlords in Mayo, both resident and absentee, were either unable or unwilling to pay these rates, as the fall off in rents during the Famine period left many of them in financial difficulties. Lord Palmer, with lands in Westport union in the parishes of Islandeady and Aughagower, was listed as a defaulting ratepayer by the Westport poor law guardians in 1848. In February of that year, he was listed as owing £223 10s. 1d. to the union, as was the marquis of Sligo who owed £1,595, and Lord Lucan who owed £317.[18] By March 1848, Lord Palmer's level of indebtedness to the Westport union had increased to £310 8s. 4d. and the guardians issued legal proceedings against him for recovery of arrears and poor rates.[19]

In 1848, the potato crop failed again. In Ballysakeery parish, which contained seven townlands from the Palmer estate, the parish priest wrote that the level of distress was worsening and that people from his parish had been forced to level their cabins and shelter in ditches in an effort to gain admittance to the Ballina workhouse.[20] In April 1848, Fr Peter Ward of Aughagower wrote:

> Our misery and sufferings are beyond measure; upwards of 1,300 dead in this abandoned and neglected parish within the past fourteen months out of a population of 6,700, and our sad prospects this day appear more awful and gloomy than ever. Famine. Pestilence. Swellings. Despair. Eighty-four children died of measles in the past twelve days all under five years of age ... In many villages the houses are levelled to the ground and people

are wandering about without indoor relief, they are frightful spectres to behold.[21]

Later that year, in its editorial dated 7 September 1848, the *Tyrawley Herald* commented:

> Another famine threatens to seize us in its deadly embrace – another year of horrors lies before our agonizing gaze. The potato crop is materially injured if not actually destroyed … we have nothing but the most appalling future to look to.[22]

The successive potato crop failures had a major impact on the population of the Palmer estates. Not only was the population size disrupted, the Famine also impacted upon the normal life and customs of the population of the Palmer property. In the Catholic parish of Islandeady for instance, which contained 40 townlands belonging to the Palmer estate, the marriage rate fell dramatically as Famine conditions grew more severe, as shown in figure 5:

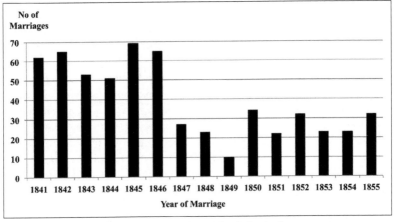

5. Number of marriages in the parish of Islandeady, 1841–55[23]

These figures are revealing for a number of reasons. In the years preceding the Famine, marriages in the parish exceeded 50 per annum, peaking at 69 marriages in 1845, the first year of the potato crop failure. Early marriage was commonplace in many parts of Mayo before the Famine as there were often few restraints on the subdivision of holdings, so small farmers were not inclined to wait for an inheritance before marrying.[24] This trend was noticeable in peasant marriages elsewhere. For instance, in Ballykilcline, Co. Roscommon, cottier-labourers were more likely to marry at an early age compared to larger farmers. Those marrying youngest were tenants-at-will with holdings of between five and 12 acres.[25]

It can be argued that marriage rates, to an extent, are a reflection of economic conditions as well as people's expectations about the future, so the high number of marriages in 1846 possibly indicates that the people of Islandeady, having experienced crop failure on previous occasions, did not believe that a consecutive series of failures was likely to happen. The failure of the potato crop in 1846 and in the following years however had a major impact on the number of marriages and the marriage rate fell significantly with only 10 marriages taking place in 1849. Indeed, in 1848, the parish priest of Islandeady wrote that 15 to 20 people were dying each day in his parish from actual starvation.[26] In the early 1850s the marriage rate increased again but never recovered to its pre-Famine level, probably because the population had declined significantly.

The marriage figures for this parish are also illuminating in other respects. By analysing the monthly marriage figures over the same period, it is possible to gain an insight into the religious customs and beliefs of the people of Islandeady and how the Famine impacted on these customs. Table 1 shows the monthly marriage statistics for Islandeady over the period 1841–54.

Table 1. Monthly marriage statistics, Islandeady, 1841–54[27]

	1841	1842	1843	1844	1845	1846	1847	1848	1849	1850	1851	1852	1853	1854
Jan.	5	7	7	15	20	10	3	4	0	6	5	1	5	5
Feb.	27	24	26	16	19	27	6	4	0	9	4	6	12	12
Mar.	8	8	1	4	6	12	6	4	1	1	4	2	1	1
Apr.	3	0	4	3	2	7	3	3	0	2	4	5	1	1
May	3	9	0	1	1	2	1	0	1	3	1	2	0	0
Jun.	5	4	2	0	4	1	0	0	0	1	0	3	1	1
Jul.	0	1	1	1	1	0	2	0	0	1	0	2	0	0
Aug.	0	0	5	0	2	0	2	1	1	3	0	1	0	0
Sept.	3	0	0	1	4	2	0	2	2	1	0	2	1	1
Oct.	1	4	4	3	0	2	3	2	2	1	1	0	0	
Nov.	7	5	3	2	5	3	0	2	2	4	1	6	1	1
Dec.	0	3	0	4	2	1	2	0	1	1	2	1	1	1

The returns show that February was the most important month for marriages in this parish. The Lenten period, traditionally associated with abstinence, was a period in which marriages were rarely contracted. As a result the period leading up to Lent, in particular shrove Tuesday, was a traditional time for weddings in many parts of the country.[28] Hence the marriage figures also help to illustrate the significance of religion and religious customs to the people on this part of the Palmer estate and the decline of February marriages during the Famine period is therefore of great significance, illustrating as it does the fact that during the Famine, normal life and customs were suspended.

February marriages increased from 19 in 1845 to 27 in 1846, again illustrating the belief among the people that the crop failure was a temporary phenomenon. However, the subsequent crop failure that year, and the harsh winter of 1846–7 had a major impact on the February marriage rate, which declined to six in 1847, four in 1848 and none in 1849. The subsequent rise in the February rate from 1850 onwards demonstrated a slow return to normality after the Famine period.

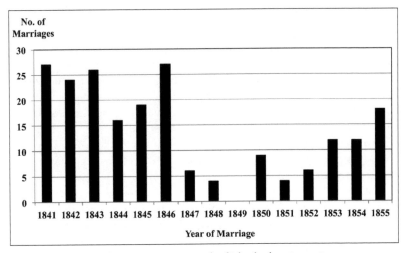

6. February marriages, parish of Islandeady, 1841–55[29]

In contrast to the social disruption experienced by the Catholic population of Islandeady, the Famine does not appear to have impacted to the same extent on the members of the Established Church. The number of Church of Ireland baptisms recorded for the parish of Aughaval, which contained 10 townlands belonging to the Palmer estates, does not show the same dramatic decline as the Islandeady marriage rate:

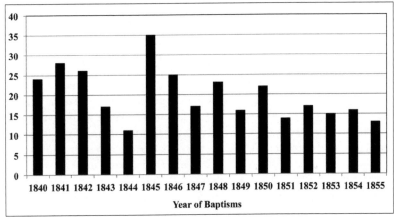

7. Church of Ireland baptisms in the parish of Aughaval, 1840–55[30]

Figure 7 demonstrates that the number of baptisms in this parish gradually rather than dramatically declined during and immediately after the Famine although the impact of the Famine on baptisms is apparent earlier than at Islandeady where marriages increased between 1845 and 1846. The lower level of social disruption to the members of the Established Church can perhaps be explained by the diversity of occupation of the parents of children being baptized. These included weavers, servants, land agents, coastguard officers, policemen, soldiers, clerks and merchants as well as farmers.[31] As such, this congregation were probably less dependent on agriculture than the majority of the Catholic population and were in a better position to survive the potato crop failure. The decline in baptisms after 1845 might however indicate that this section of the community was initially more sensitive to crop failure, as many were merchants who depended on the expenditure of farmers for their income.

It is also possible to measure the demographic impact of the Famine on the wider population of Palmer's Mayo estates. In each of the five baronies containing Palmer land, there was significant population decline during this period. By comparing the census figures for each barony with the returns for the Palmer properties in each barony, it is possible to compare and contrast the decline in population between the Palmer estates and the county overall.

The largest portion of the Palmer estates in Mayo were in the barony of Tirawley where Lord Palmer owned 50,841 acres in the 1840s.[32] In 1841, the total male population of the Tirawley properties was 5,167 with a female population of 5,169 giving an overall total of 10,336 persons. By 1851 the male population had declined to 2,712 and the female population had fallen to 2,884, giving a total population of 5,596, a decline of 4,740 persons over the 10-year period.[33] In percentage terms, the male population fell by 48 per cent and the female population declined by 44 per cent giving an overall decrease of 46 per cent in 10 years.

An examination of the data for the individual townlands reveals some significant variations on different parts of the Tirawley estate. Despite the overall large reduction in the size of the population in the period bridging the Great Famine, thirteen townlands actually recorded an increase in their population during this period.

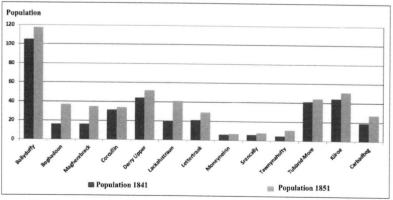

8. Townlands recording a population increase, Palmer Tirawley estate, 1841–51[34]

Significantly, each of these townlands had a population density of less than one person per acre and the average population density of these townlands was only 0.13 persons per acre in 1841. Also significant is the fact that nine of these townlands – Boghadoon, Corcullin, Derry Upper, Lackalustraun, Lettertrask, Moneyneirin, Srancally, Tawnynahulty and Tubbrid-More – are situated immediately beside or in close proximity to each other on poorly drained bogland to the south of Crossmolina. Five of these nine townlands recorded an increase in the number of occupied houses as the population increased. Three townlands – Moneyneirin, where the population increase was one person, Srancally, where the population increase was two persons and Tubbrid-More, where the population grew by three persons – recorded no change in the number of occupied houses. Only Corcullin, which recorded a population increase of three persons, experienced a decline in the number of occupied houses from five to three.[35] The general trend in housing would therefore seem to confirm that the small increase in population recorded for these nine townlands was matched by a small overall increase on the number of occupied houses.

An examination of the maps accompanying the 1840s valuation survey of the Palmer estates shows that those townlands recording a population increase contained small amounts of arable land, very few trees, and large tracts of bog, often with lakes of varying sizes dotting the landscape, an indication of the poor drainage and wet climate of this area. The townlands named above contained very little settlement or evidence of cultivation with only Tubbrid-More and Derry Upper showing evidence of clustered settlement with infields marked adjacent to these clusters. In the townland of Derry Upper the land is recorded as being held in the names of Widow Rowland, Michael and Patrick Rowland, John Kilker and Patrick Hogan. These tenants are given the title of co-partners. The valuation map for this townland also contains a corn kiln beside the settlement, providing an indication that crops other than potatoes were grown in the vicinity of the settlement.[36] The small extent of cultivated land in those townlands recording an increase in population between 1841 and 1851 can probably therefore be attributed to the adverse environmental conditions as well as the lack of an adequate labour force to carry out the labour-intensive task of reclaiming marginal land.

The low population density of these townlands in 1841 may have facilitated an expanding population. Alternatively, the nature of the terrain may have been a factor that attracted migrants to these townlands. In other regions of better soil quality, landlords and their agents took the opportunity to strip the land, breaking up rundale settlement and reducing the population density in these regions in the process.[37] Evidence of striping on the Palmer estates can be found by examining the maps accompanying the valuation survey of the Palmer estate. In many townlands, such as at Gortskeddia and Gortanedaen in the barony of Tirawley, these estate maps clearly illustrate a planned landscape rather than one divided into clachans, infields and outfields.[38] Tenants from these regions may have moved to marginal land where striping was very difficult. It is possible that Lord Palmer allowed the population of these townlands to expand as a deliberate matter of policy. Kevin Whelan has postulated that landlords encouraged the creation of rundale villages on marginal parts of their properties as rental income from partnership tenants was efficiently paid, marginal land was brought into cultivation, an outlet was provided for surplus displaced tenants and contentious issues such as turbary rights and communal grazing were regulated locally by the tenants themselves.[39]

Despite the increase in population recorded in the above townlands, the Palmer Tirawley estates in general suffered massive population decline in many areas. In the parish of Lackan for instance, the population of the townland of Ballymurphy fell from 87 persons in 1841 to just five persons in 1851, a decline of 94 per cent. The population of Barnhall Upper in the same parish declined from 237 in 1841 to 66 in 1851, a fall of 72 per cent. Similarly, the townland of Carrowmore experienced a reduction in population from 152 in 1841 to 38 in 1851, a decline of 75 per cent.[40]

In the parish of Templemurry, the townland of Rathnawooraun with 110 occupants in 1841 was devoid of population in 1851. The nearby townlands of Rathfranpark and Tooracappul experienced the same fate with a 100 per cent decrease in population recorded in these townlands.[41]

An examination of the demographic trends for the barony of Tirawley as a whole between 1841 and 1851 reveals a decline in the male population of 40 per cent and a fall in the female population of 36 per cent; yielding an overall reduction of 38 per cent. The Palmer lands in this barony recorded a population decline of 46 per cent. These figures clearly demonstrate a significantly greater fall in population for the Palmer estates than elsewhere in the barony of Tirawley.

The barony of Burrishoole is situated in the south-west of the county (see figure 4). Lord Palmer rented out 5,300 acres of his Burrishoole estate in 45 different townlands in the 1840s.[42] In 1841, the total male population of the Burrishoole property was 2,238 and the female population was 2,195, giving a total population of 4,433 persons, equivalent to 19 per cent of Palmer's Mayo tenants in 1841. By 1851 the male population had been reduced to 1,277 whilst the female population had declined to 1,384, giving a total population of 2,661, a reduction of 1,772 persons over this 10-year period.[43] In percentage terms this corresponds to a fall in the male population of 43 per cent and a fall in the female population of 37 per cent, giving an overall decrease of 40 per cent.

As with the Tirawley estate, there were some notable statistical variations on this part of the property also. Four of the townlands in the Burrishoole estate – Keeloges, Derrycreeve, Drumminahaha and Ranaghy – recorded an increase in population between 1841 and 1851, although the net gain in population for these four townlands was only 47 persons. As with the Tirawley portion of the Palmer lands, these townlands were located in close proximity to each other near Islandeady Lough which is roughly equidistant from Westport and Castlebar.

The general population trend for the Burrishoole property was however one of significant population decline. In Gortnafahy townland in the parish of Burrishoole the male population declined by 10 whereas the female population fell by 47, a significant differential. This might possibly indicate a higher rate of emigration among females in this townland. The townland of Ardagh in the same parish saw its population decline from 69 persons in 1841 to just seven persons in 1851, a reduction of 90 per cent. The townland of Cornagaslaun in the parish of Islandeady recorded a decline from 200 persons in 1841 to 67 in 1851, a decrease of 67 per cent over the 10-year period.[44]

Census figures for the barony of Burrishoole in its entirety show that the population declined by 38 per cent between 1841 and 1851. On the Palmer estates in this barony, the population decreased by 40 per cent so the rate of decline in the townlands of the Palmer property was slightly higher than the average decline for the barony as a whole.

The barony of Murrisk is situated in the south-west of Co. Mayo (see figure 4). Lord Palmer rented out 3,247 acres in 10 townlands in this barony in the 1840s.[45] In 1841 there were 646 males and 593 females residing on this portion of the estate giving a total population on 1,239. By 1851, the male population was 377 and the female population was 386 giving a total population of 763, a reduction of 476 during this period.[46] In percentage terms, the male population on the Palmer Murrisk lands fell by 42 per cent while the female population declined by 35 per cent, giving an overall reduction of 38 per cent.

Within the townlands of the Murrisk estate, there were significant demographic variations. Three townlands – Cartoor, Furgill and Kilsallagh Upper – recorded population decline of more than 50 per cent between 1841 and 1851. Two townlands – Gorteendarragh and Drummin West – recorded a rise in population. Gorteendarragh however was unoccupied in 1841 and only contained two inhabitants by 1851. Drummin West recorded an increase in its population from 72 in 1841 to 84 by 1851, an overall increase of 17 per cent.

The census figures for the barony of Murrisk overall show that the population declined from 34,402 to 24,992 between 1841 and 1851, a decline of 27 per cent. The decline on the Palmer estate in this barony was much higher at 38 per cent, mirroring the pattern from the barony of Tirawley.

The barony of Gallen is located to the east of Co. Mayo (see figure 4). In this barony, Lord Palmer rented over 5,100 acres in the 1840s.[47] The Palmer property consisted of 28 townlands and contained 2,002 males and 1,948 females in 1841, a total of 3,950 persons. By 1851 the number of males had declined to 1,250 and the number of females had fallen to 1,290, a total of 2,540 occupants, giving an overall decline of 1,410 occupants, equivalent to a 36 per cent decline in the population on the Palmer estates.[48]

As with other parts of the Palmer estates, there were notable demographic variations between townlands on the Gallen estate. Out of the total of 28 townlands, three recorded an increase in population between 1841 and 1851. These townlands were Castleroyan with a 16 per cent increase, Tawnabeg with a 236 per cent increase and Cloondoolough with an 11 per cent increase. The total increase in population for these townlands in numerical terms was 176 persons. Unlike the other baronies where clusters of townlands recorded a population increase, these three townlands were geographically dispersed from each other. The census figures for the barony as a whole show that the total population declined by 26 per cent whereas the decline in the population of the Palmer Gallen estate was significantly higher at 36 per cent.

The barony of Carra is situated in the south of the county (see figure 4). The Palmer estates in this barony consisted of over 6,500 acres situated in 19 different townlands, all in the parish of Islandeady.[49] None of these townlands recorded an increase in population between 1841 and 1851. The total male population in 1841 was 1,466. The female population that year was recorded at 1,427 giving a total of 2,893 persons. By 1851 the male population had declined to 782 and the female population on this estate had decreased to 770, yielding a total of 1,552. This equates to a fall in population of 1,341 persons. In percentage terms, the population of the Palmer Carra property declined by 46 per cent, the largest percentage decline recorded in any of the five baronies in which the Palmer estates were situated.

Several townlands on this estate suffered a dramatic decrease in population. For instance, the townland of Bohehs lost 86 per cent of its population between 1841 and 1851. The population of the townland of Lappalagh declined by 78 per cent and Knockbaun experienced a decrease of 71 per cent in its population. In Bohehs, house numbers declined by 89 per cent. In Lappalagh, house numbers fell by 82 per cent and in Knockbaun, house numbers decreased by 67 per cent. The decline in population on this part of the estate was therefore matched by a similar decline in the number of occupied houses, indicating that the census returns can generally be regarded as accurate in this instance. For the barony as a whole the population decreased by 37 per cent, a figure significantly lower than the 46 per cent recorded for the Palmer estate in this barony.[50]

The Mayo estates of Lord Palmer experienced a dramatic decline in population and house numbers between 1841 and 1851. The rate of decline on the Palmer property in each of the five baronies was greater than the decrease recorded for the baronies overall. The rate of decrease was also significantly higher than that for the entire county.

These census figures clearly demonstrate that population decline on the Palmer estates between 1841 and 1851 was not only substantial, it was significantly higher than that for the county as a whole. It is necessary therefore to examine the reasons for this decline and to establish why conditions on the

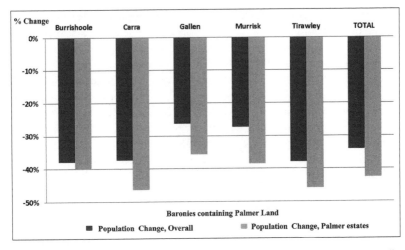

9. Population change by barony, 1841–51, Palmer estates compared with baronies overall[51]

Palmer property would seem to have been harsher than those that prevailed in Mayo generally during this period.

The rapid decline in the population of the Palmer estates during the period 1841–51 can be attributed to a combination of ejectments, migration and death by starvation or disease. There is significant evidence to suggest that Lord Palmer ejected tenants on a large scale, principally for economic reasons, during the Famine period. The 'Alphabethical register of leases of the Mayo estates of Sir W.H. Palmer' contains details on most of the leases issued by the Palmer family in Co. Mayo.[52] This register records details about the nature and type

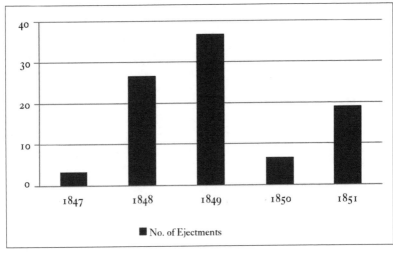

10. Ejectment of leaseholders, Palmer Mayo estates, 1847–51[53]

of leases as well as observations by Lord Palmer's agent Francis O'Donnell about ejectment of leaseholders. Out of a total of 431 leases in this register, 106 leaseholders were evicted, a figure equivalent to 24 per cent of all leases issued by the Palmer estate. Many of these leases were issued jointly or in common so the actual number of persons evicted was substantial. Of these evictions, 92 occurred between 1847 and 1851, during the height of the Famine, as shown in figure 10.

The vast majority of the tenants on the Palmer estates did not hold leases but were tenants at will,[54] renting their land with far less security of tenure than leaseholders.

Further evidence about evictions from the Palmer lands can be obtained from returns of notices served upon the relieving officers of the poor law districts in Ireland.[55] For instance the 1849 returns for Co. Mayo (the first year in which these returns were made) detail the evictions of tenants by Thomas Ormsby, Sir William Palmer's agent. Table 2 summarizes the eviction statistics for the Palmer Mayo property for that year.

Table 2. Number of persons evicted from the Palmer Mayo estates, 1849[56]

Townland	Numbers Evicted
Gurrard	36
Rooskey	24
Baranarran	4
Glenedagh	22
Rinmore	7
Farrinascullogh	11
Cloonagh & Knockanello	12
Gurteen	18
Laghtamacdurkan	12
Total	146

In reality the numbers evicted were probably much greater than 146 persons, as in some cases the returns refer to the number of families evicted rather than to individuals. Given that the average family size at this time was six or seven persons,[57] evictions from the Palmer estates could possibly have numbered well over 1,000 people.

By comparing these eviction figures with the population of the above townlands in 1841, the contribution of evictions to the decline in population in these areas between 1841 and 1851 can, to an extent, be estimated. For instance, the population of Roosky in Tirawley numbered 199 persons in 1841 but had declined to just 59 persons by 1851, a fall of 70 per cent.[58] If the eviction statistics for this townland are just for individuals rather than families, evictions contributed to 17 per cent of the decline in population of Roosky in the year 1849 alone. If the eviction returns contain some families then evictions played an even greater part in this decline in population.

Evictions undoubtedly played a significant part in the population decline on the Palmer property. Evictions frequently occurred because of non-payment of rent. Lord Palmer was clearly concerned about the fall off in rent payments on his Mayo estate when he wrote to the lord lieutenant to request that a police station be established in the parish of Islandeady to provide help to his agent to collect rents in his locality.[59] However, in addition to the contraction of his rental income, Lord Palmer was faced with escalating expenses when the burden of financing relief efforts was transferred to landlords in 1847 by the government who abolished the public works scheme and obliged landlords to pay rates for those tenants with a rateable valuation of £4 or less. The increase in evictions from the Palmer estates after 1847 can possibly be attributed to these factors.

The failure of the potato crop not only left many of Palmer's tenants unable to pay their rents, it left many of them destitute, homeless and starving. There is no doubt that the massive population decline on the Palmer property and elsewhere in Mayo can to a great extent be attributed to death by starvation or by disease directly related to the Famine conditions. Catholic burial registers are not available for this period so the exact number of deaths on the Palmer estates is impossible to quantify. However, it is possible to obtain an indication of the increase in the death rate by examining the burial registers of the Established Church in Mayo. The records from Aughaval, though incomplete, show that deaths among their parishioners rose substantially during the Famine period:

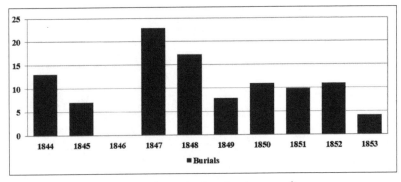

11. Burials, parish of Aughaval, 1844–53[60]
(No burials are recorded for 1846)

The peak years for burials in this parish were 1847 and 1848. The number of burials recorded in this parish in 1847 was 23 compared with just seven in 1845. Taking 1845 as a base year for comparative purposes, this equates to an increase in burials of 328 per cent over this two-year period. In 1848, the number of burials had fallen to 17, a figure still 242 per cent higher than the 1845 total. It is probable that the death rate among Catholic smallholders and labourers was even higher, given their greater dependence on agriculture.

It was against this background of misery and destitution that evictions of tenants from the Palmer estates were taking place. Lord Palmer however was by no means unique in behaving in this fashion. Lord Lucan for instance, with large properties around Castlebar and Ballinrobe, used the opportunity presented by the Famine to implement a policy of widespread evictions in order to make his property more profitable. 10,000 people were evicted from the region around Ballinrobe and 15,000 acres were cleared in the district. Around Castlebar, several populous villages were completely destroyed and large farms created in their place.[61] The evidence for the Palmer estates however would suggest that evictions during the Famine period were for non-payment of rent[62] and were not necessarily part of an agriculture plan to remodel holdings and to create more economic grazing farms as was the case on the Lucan property.[63]

Other landlords behaved in a similar fashion, carrying out evictions during the Famine period. Henry Joynt, the agent of Lord Arran, evicted at least 85 people from around Crossmolina in 1849. George Clendining, the agent of Sir R.A. O'Donnell, evicted at least 16 people from the townland of Rosduane, near Westport, in the same year.[64]

Part of the depopulation of the Palmer Mayo property can be attributed to emigration, either by tenants who had been ejected or who had surrendered their holdings to flee to Britain and America. The level of migration from the Palmer Mayo estates is unknown as no adequate county-based statistics on emigration are available before 1851. Estimates for Mayo emigration during the Famine vary from 50,000 to 70,000 persons – a figure equivalent to 40 per cent of the county's Famine population loss.[65] The population of the Palmer Mayo property fell from 22,851 in 1841 to 13,112 in 1851, a fall of 9,739 persons.[66] If this estimated emigration level for Mayo generally is applied to Palmer lands, then emigration accounted for the loss of over 4,200 persons. However, there is no way to be certain if emigration levels for the Palmer property were equivalent to the county average. Indeed, they may have been lower, as many tenants would have difficulty affording the fare of between 50s. and 75s. to America. In consequence, much of the emigration was selective, with the relatively well-off migrating in large numbers, a point made by Captain Farren of the Castlebar poor law union board of guardians:

> The trades people have also been affected by the badness of the times, rendering them less able to meet their burdens; many have left the country

for America, and some of the more comfortable class of small farmers have followed their example.[67]

The reasons for the enormous decline in population on the Palmer estates between 1841 and 1851 are therefore numerous, integrated and complex. The absence of a resident landlord, the lack of incentives to improve holdings, the small size of holdings due to the subdivision of farms which left many in a precarious economic position, the role of middlemen and agents, the repeated failure of the potato crop, evictions and distraining, poverty, migration, disease and starvation, misguided government policies – all played their part in the dramatic demographic decline on the Palmer estates during this period.

3. Politics, evictions and the post-Famine economic recovery on the Palmer estates

The demographic decline on the Palmer estates triggered by the Famine continued during the 1850s, although the rate of decline slowed down substantially with an overall population reduction on Palmer's Mayo estates between 1851 and 1861 of 12 per cent.[1] In the barony of Tirawley, some townlands managed to reverse the population decline recorded during the Famine period and recorded an increase in population. For instance, in the parish of Addergoole, which contained nine townlands belonging to the Palmer estates, the townland of Carrowkeel, which had experienced a decline in population of 94 per cent between 1841 and 1851, recorded a growth in population of 517 per cent between 1851 and 1861. Similarly, the townland of Carrockbarret in the same parish with a population decline of 57 per cent in the 1840s recorded population growth of 33 per cent in the following decade, while the townland of Prughlish reversed a decline of 79 per cent between 1841 and 1851 to record growth of 240 per cent between 1851 and 1861.

Elsewhere in this parish however, this trend was not sustained. Ballyduffy townland, which actually experienced a population increase of 10 per cent in the 1840s, suffered a fall in its population of 26 per cent between 1851 and 1861. Ballyknock, which recorded a decline in its population of 32 per cent between 1841 and 1851, experienced a further fall of 41 per cent during the 1850s. Doonaroya's population, which fell by 15 per cent during the 1840s, fell by a further 6 per cent during the next decade.

In the nearby parish of Crossmolina, a similar mixed pattern can be identified. Of the eight townlands belonging to the Palmer estate that actually recorded an increase in population during the Famine, six continued to grow during the 1850s. For instance, the population of the townland of Lettertrask, which had grown by 32 per cent in the 1840s, increased by a further 28 per cent during the 1850s while Moneyneirin townland, which had grown by 17 per cent in the 1840s, managed to increase its population size from seven persons in 1851 to 34 in 1861, a percentage increase of 386 per cent. However, in Tawnynahulty, where the population had grown by 84 per cent during the Famine, numbers fell away in the 1850s and the population declined by 64 per cent.

In overall terms, 37 townlands on the Tirawley estate experienced population growth between 1851 and 1861, compared with just 13 townlands during the 1840s. The population of the Tirawley part of the Palmer estates however declined from 5,596 persons to 4,736 persons between 1851 and 1861, a decrease of 15 per cent. In the preceding decade, the population of the Tirawley estate had declined by 46 per cent so the very rapid population decline had been arrested but not eliminated. For the barony of Tirawley overall, the population declined from 44,195 in 1851 to 38,787 in 1861, a percentage fall of 12 per cent, so the pattern of the previous decade, whereby higher than average population decline was recorded on the Palmer Tirawley estate, was repeated.

In the barony of Burrishoole, where population size had declined on the Palmer estate by 40 per cent between 1841 and 1851, further substantial decreases in population were recorded. The population of the townland of Kilbree Lower in the parish of Ballintober fell from 200 in 1851 to just eight in 1861, a decline of 96 per cent. In Burrishoole parish, Caulicaun townland, with a population of 14 in 1851, Rusheens, with a population of ten in 1851 and Lisduff, with a population of 30 in 1851, were all devoid of population by 1861. Out of a total of 46 townlands on this part of the Palmer estate only eight townlands recorded a population increase during this period, and in overall terms the entire population of the Burrishoole estate fell from 2,661 persons in 1851 to 1,971 persons in 1861; a 26 per cent decrease during the decade.[2]

This high rate of population decline in Tirawley and Burrishoole was not however matched on other parts of the Palmer estates. In the barony of Carra, where the population of the Palmer estate had fallen by 46 per cent between 1841 and 1851, the population decline was arrested during the following decade with only a 1 per cent decline in population recorded. Similarly, on the Palmer Murrisk estate, where the population size had fallen by 38 per cent during the 1840s, a further small decrease of 2 per cent occurred during the 1850s. On the Gallen portion of the Palmer estate, the population actually grew slightly between 1851 and 1861. The increase in population of 2 per cent contrasted sharply with the 38 per cent fall in population numbers in this barony during the preceding decade.

Table 3 shows the overall population trends between 1841 and 1861 in each of the five baronies in which Lord Palmer held land:

Table 3. Demographic change in five Mayo baronies, 1841–61[3]

Barony	Population			% Change	
	1841	1851	1861	1841–51	1851–61
Burrishoole	39,858	24,753	21,520	-38%	-13%
Carra	52,238	32,707	28,647	-37%	-12%
Gallen	46,566	34,336	37,695	-26%	+10%
Murrisk	34,402	24,992	19,332	-27%	-23%
Tirawley	71,232	44,195	38,787	-38%	-12%
Total	244,296	160,983	145,981	-34%	-9%

The population changes on the Palmer estates in each of these baronies varied considerably with the overall figures. In Tirawley and Burrishoole, the population decline between 1851 and 1861 was greater on the Palmer estates than in the baronies overall. In Carra and Murrisk, the decline on the Palmer estates was substantially less than for those baronies overall during the same period. In Gallen, where the population of the Palmer estate had risen by 2 per cent between 1851 and 1861, the population of the entire barony increased as well but at a substantially faster rate than on the Palmer estate. Nevertheless, the overall trend of a slower decrease in population size when compared to the previous decade points to a slowly improving economic situation during the 1850s, a recovery triggered by the Crimean war which had boosted the price of many agricultural products in the mid-1850s. This improvement would seem to have been patchy, occurring at different rates in different regions of Mayo, with many areas still experiencing severe difficulties in the post-Famine period.

Significant improvements in agricultural output were recorded in those Mayo unions that contained Palmer lands during the 1850s. These improvements occurred in both the tillage and livestock sectors. Table 4 contrasts the levels of output in potatoes and livestock in the Ballina and Castlebar unions between 1847, in the middle of the Famine period, and 1856, after the outbreak of the Crimean war. Ballina union contained the parishes of Crossmolina, Lacken, Killala, Ballysakeery and Attymas where much of the Palmer estates were located. Castlebar union included the parishes of Islandeady and Addergoole which also contained extensive Palmer territories.

Table 4. Agricultural statistics for 1847 and 1856, Ballina and Castlebar unions[4]

District	Acreage of Potatoes	Quantity of Potatoes (20 Stone Barrels)	Number of Cattle	Number of Pigs	Number of Sheep
Ballina Union 1847	1,834	82,530	23,056	2,623	20,779
Ballina Union 1856	9,672	292,592	18,455	4,450	25,143
% Change	**427%**	**255%**	**-20%**	**70%**	**21%**
Castlebar Union 1847	803	35,493	12,591	1,195	15,647
Castlebar Union 1856	8,738	279,684	20,711	4,163	37,342
% Change	**988%**	**688%**	**64%**	**248%**	**139%**

These figures clearly point to a significant improvement in agricultural output in 1856 compared with the Famine period. In Ballina union, potato output had increased by 255 per cent while in the Castlebar union, output had risen by 688 per cent. Large gains were also made in other sectors with the exception of the number of cattle in the Ballina union which declined by 20 per cent over this time period. However, during the 1850s, livestock prices continued to rise, boosting the post-Famine economic recovery in Mayo. Table 5 lists the value of livestock in the county between 1852 and 1856:

Table 5. Value of livestock, Co. Mayo, 1852–6[5]

	1852	1853	1854	1855	1856
Value of Livestock in Mayo	£1,254,514	£1,410,273	£1,521,840	£1,518,065	£1,568,506

For the county as a whole, cattle numbers increased from 79,148 in 1847 to 158,774 by 1856 while potato production rose from 366,468 barrels in 1847 to 2,109,547 barrels by 1856.[6] The increase in agricultural output and prices in the 1850s therefore points to a significant economic recovery in the post-Famine period on the Palmer estates and the county in general.

Further evidence for the post-Famine economic recovery can be obtained from an examination of rentals from the Palmer Mayo estates in the early 1860s. The rent book for the period 1 November 1862 to 1 May 1863 shows that out of a total listed tenantry of 1,418 persons, only 15 were in arrears by 1 May 1863, a substantial indication of improved economic conditions (see Table 6). On the Burrishoole property only three out of 302 tenants were in arrears. In Carra, every one of the 122 tenants had paid their rent fully, something the 117 tenants on the Murrisk estate also managed to do. In Gallen, four out of 243 tenants were in arrears whilst in Tirawley, the largest section of the property, eight out of 634 tenants owed rent on 1 May 1863.

Table 6. Rentals for the Palmer Mayo estates, 1 Nov. 1862–1 May 1863[7]

Barony	Tenant Numbers	Arrears due on 1 Nov. 1862 £ - s. - d.	Half years rent and rent due, 1 May 1863 £ - s. - d.	Total Rent Charge and arrears due, 1 May 1863 £ - s. - d.	Amount Received thereof £ - s. - d.	Amount of Arrears 1 May 1863 £ - s. - d.
Burrishoole	302	10 - 1 - 6	1,337 - 16 - 0	1,347 - 17 - 6	1,318 - 13 - 6	29 - 4 - 0
Carra	122	---	714 - 6 - 3	714 - 6 - 3	714 - 6 - 3	---
Gallen	243	76 - 8 - 7	1,598 - 5 - 3	1,674 - 13 - 11	1,579 - 17 - 9	94 - 16 - 2
Murrisk	117	---	266 - 15 - 0	266 - 15 - 0	266 - 15 - 0	---
Tirawley	634	74 - 14 - 7	3,888 - 10 - 4	3,963 - 4 - 11	3,759 - 3 - 8	204 - 1 - 3

The total half-year's rent due from the Mayo lands came to £7,805, of which £328 was unpaid, a figure equivalent to only 4 per cent of rentals. This low level of indebtedness throughout the Mayo estates is further evidence of prosperity and recovery after the Famine.

The pattern of landholding that existed on the Palmer Mayo estates appears to have survived the Famine period broadly intact. Although the population had substantially declined, the system of letting and subletting of land still prevailed in several townlands. This is reflected in the predominance of potatoes and pig production (see Table 4), characteristic of a small farm economy. In the parish of Lackan in the 1850s, lands in the townland of Aghaleague were leased to the Reverend William Bourke of the Church Education Society who held 129 acres for his own use and in turn sublet 574 acres to 29 tenants in nine holdings ranging in size from ten acres to 95 acres. In the same parish, land in the townland of Cloonanass was also sublet by William Bourke to five tenants in two different holdings.[8]

In the townland of Mungaun, to the south of Crossmolina, Walter Bourke sublet lands amounting to 577 acres to Pat Gallagher who in turn leased three acres to Dominick Gallagher. Richard Gallagher who leased 362 acres from Walter Bourke in turn sublet six acres to Anthony Scanlan. In the nearby townland of Lackalustrane, Patrick O'Boyle, who was leasing 372 acres from Lord Palmer, in turn sublet three acres to Henry Barrett. However, the vast majority of the tenants on the Palmer properties in the mid-1850s appear to have leased their land directly from the estate rather than from middlemen. In the parish of Lackan for instance, Sir Roger was the only listed lessor for the townlands of Barnhill Upper, Barroe, Billous, Carrickanass, Carrowkilleen and Carrowmore, an area exceeding 1,500 acres.[9] Therefore the pre-Famine landholding structures whereby a small number of leaseholders sublet land while the vast majority existed without leases seems to have remained in place during the 1850s.

The overall decline in the population of the Palmer Mayo estates during the 1850s can therefore be attributed to a number of factors. In the early part of the decade, evictions and surrendering of holdings continued, possibly indicating that famine conditions continued into this period. The rise in agricultural prices, particularly those for livestock, would have encouraged consolidation and a switch from tillage to pasture. Continued emigration from Mayo during the 1850s also reduced the population size. Between 1 May 1851 and 31 December 1857 an estimated 24,343 people, or 9 per cent of Mayo's 1851 population, emigrated. This figure, though appearing initially to be high, was in fact low when compared with other counties. During the same time period, Tipperary lost 21 per cent of its population through emigration while 13 per cent of Galway's population left the country. Mayo's level of emigration was actually the third lowest of any county with only Sligo and Dublin experiencing a lower emigration rate.[10]

The large-scale eviction of tenants from the Palmer estates during the Famine was directly attributable to the potato crop failure which in turn caused economic difficulties which resulted in many tenants being unable to pay their rents. In the 1850s the rate of evictions on the Palmer estates for this reason declined significantly (only five evictions of leaseholders were recorded between 1853 and 1868),[11] demonstrating that a post-Famine economic recovery enabled most tenants to pay their rents. This economic recovery therefore resulted in the restoration of the pre-Famine economic order on the Palmer estates. However, the Famine period and its immediate aftermath had also resulted in profound social and political disruption, a fact demonstrated by the controversial events on the Palmer estate following the 1852 Mayo election.

Lord Palmer, in common with many of his contemporaries, believed that owning land conferred on him the right to dictate to his tenants how they should vote at election times. Despite being an absentee, he took an active interest in Mayo politics and issued voting instructions to his tenants. The handing down of election orders, often through the medium of agents, was widely practised by many landlords. In the Clare election of 1852, the landlords supporting the Tory candidate were asked to give a free vote to their tenants but only three complied.[12] Colonel Bruen was criticized in 1835 for evicting tenants in Carlow on electoral grounds and Lord Powerscourt admitted that all landlords used force at Wicklow elections.[13] The agent of Lord Palmer, Thomas Ormsby, and his sub-agent Francis O'Donnell, visited the freeholders on the Palmer property before the 1852 election to advise them to vote for Colonel McAlpine.[14]

Colonel McAlpine's candidature was opposed by the Catholic clergy. In 1850, the Tory government had introduced the Ecclesiastical Titles bill that sought to prohibit Catholic bishops from holding territorial titles in Britain. The government followed this action by issuing a proclamation on 15 June 1851 reminding Catholics that it was illegal for them to exercise the ceremonies of their religion in public or for their ecclesiastics to wear publicly the habits of their order.[15] Later that month, following a procession of Catholic schoolchildren in Stockport, England, rioting began and Catholic homes and churches were wrecked and in one church the tabernacle was broken open and the hosts spilt on the ground.[16] Catholics blamed the government for stirring up anti-Catholic feeling and bigotry and so the Mayo clergy campaigned vigorously against McAlpine, the Tory candidate. Catholic voters on the Palmer estate were placed in the invidious position of either voting as their landlord dictated and risking the wrath of their priests, or opposing McAlpine and incurring the anger of Lord Palmer.

The system of open voting at this time made coercion possible, with priests and landlord's agents usually attending the polling booths to check which way votes were cast. There were 37 freeholders on the Tirawley estate of Lord Palmer entitled to vote.[17] At least 23 of these freeholders disobeyed their landlord's instruction by either voting against Colonel McAlpine, by giving their votes to the other candidates, George Henry Moore and Ouseley Higgins, or by abstaining altogether.[18] Moore was a Catholic Mayo landlord who campaigned for tenants' rights and actively opposed the Ecclesiastical Titles bill and Higgins was a Catholic Liberal, so they were more likely to attract the Catholic vote. The tenants of Lord Palmer who voted for these candidates were Catholic in all but one case although both Catholic and Protestant tenants abstained. Pressure, intimidation, religion and fear of attack were all factors that influenced this voting pattern. Elections at this time were often rowdy affairs with rioting commonplace and the absence of a secret ballot meant that many people were intimidated on their way to the voting centres. Indeed, Francis O'Donnell, a sub-agent of Lord Palmer, had his nose broken, his pistols stolen and was temporarily imprisoned by a hostile crowd in a hotel room in Castlebar when on his way to Ballina and Crossmolina to escort tenants to the polling booth.[19]

McAlpine lost the election and 15 tenants of Lord Palmer's who either voted against McAlpine or abstained were issued with notices to quit. Some of the tenants who abstained were treated similarly whilst others escaped punishment. For instance, James McNaires and John Robertson, both Protestants who did not vote, were not punished but Martin Flanagan, a Catholic who also abstained, was served with a notice to quit.[20]

The 15 tenants who had been served with notices to quit by Thomas Ormsby petitioned Lord Palmer in January 1853 in the hope of having this decision reversed. This petition outlined the tenants' feelings of injustice at the pending evictions pointing out that they had promptly paid their rents, even during the Famine:

> That we have all been served with notices to quit, in consequence of voting at the last Mayo election against Colonel McAlpine, in some instances for not voting at all and in some instances without being asked by any party to vote one way or the other.
>
> That we have struggled during seven years of unprecedented distress.
>
> That during that trying time we paid our respective rents regularly and that at present we do not owe one farthing.
>
> That we think it a great hardship the moment there is a prospect of better times to be thrown ourselves and dependent families on the world.
>
> That memorialists believe they committed no crimes and should not be punished.
>
> That memorialists have not heard of any such punishment on the Palmer estates hitherto and humbly hope ... your honour will still continue us as your tenants.
>
> That memorialists hope ... your honour will send an early and favourable answer to Patrick Gallagher, Crossmolina, one of the memorialists.[21]

Lord Palmer replied to the memorial promptly from his home in Wales. His letter to Patrick Gallagher is revealing in that it gives an insight into his character, the management of his estate and his 'rights' as a landlord:

> Since receiving your petition, I have enquired as to the cause for which you and the rest of the petitioners received notice to quit and ... I find all

of you (with one exception) voted directly against my wishes at the last election for Mayo, thereby disobliging me as much as it was in your power to do.[22]

This statement reveals that the initial decision to evict tenants was not taken by Lord Palmer (it was in fact taken by his agent Thomas Ormsby), but he nonetheless felt annoyed that his tenants had not voted as he would have wished, a point he re-emphasized in the next passage of his letter:

> When tenants want favours or indulgences of any sort, it is always to the landlord they apply and therefore I do think that tenants on their part might make a point of following their landlord's directing at election times in preference to those of any other persons whatsoever.[23]

Having outlined his views on what he believed tenants should do at election times, he then gave his reasons for not changing the decision to eject those who did not follow his instructions:

> You and your fellow petitioners ... not only refused to vote for the candidate supported but you went dead against me and gave all your votes to the opposite party in defiance of my firm wishes and requests. Now you want me to overlook this and to forgive the way in which you set me at defiance, but I consider such conduct deserves punishment, and therefore I shall not interfere with Mr Ormsby's decision upon the subject ... those who refuse to comply with my reasonable requests, and who act in direct opposition to my wishes, can expect neither favours nor indulgences at my hands.[24]

It is possible that the proposed evictions were threatened on religious grounds. It is clear however from the vindictive tone of his letter that Lord Palmer wanted to use this opportunity to quell any dissent among his tenants and to teach those who disobeyed him a severe lesson. By his action he was also re-emphasizing what he believed was his right, to dictate to tenants how they should vote at election times. This process of serving notices to quit to disobedient tenants was not, however, exclusive to Palmer. Lord Londonderry also served a large number of ejectments and processes among those who had disobeyed his election orders in 1852.[25]

In desperation at this reply the tenants turned to George Henry Moore, MP, asking him to intervene with Lord Palmer on their behalf. In his letter to Palmer, Moore initially professed friendly greetings towards Palmer and then turned to the matter in question.

> Some of your tenants have received notices to quit in connection with their votes at the last election and in reply to their memorial you have

addressed a letter to them in which you distinctly state that the notice they received was as a punishment for their vote at the last election ... this letter might be made useful for many public purposes, but many other feelings sway me from such a course ... a very prominent one is the great reluctance which I should naturally entertain, to injure the character of an old friend like yourself and to interfere with the future of your son ... I say that the publication of such a letter in the House of Commons ... would be a duty that I should be most reluctant to discharge.[26]

Moore's threat to publish the letter and to damage the reputation of Lord Palmer was designed to change Palmer's decision to evict the 15 tenants. By early March, Moore had still received no reply and the tenants were due to be evicted. Father B. Malone, a priest in Killala where two of the petitioners, Barth Ford and Patrick Kelly, resided, wrote to Moore to see if he had any success in persuading Palmer to reverse his decision:

Have you done anything with Sir Roger Palmer on behalf of the unfortunate tenants? ... Would not his letter be a powerful document to produce before the committee that is now sitting upon the land question? Poor Ford with his weak family will be turned out next week. I don't know what I will do with him.[27]

Lord Palmer eventually replied to Moore at the end of March. Again, he refused to change his decision to evict the tenants in question and did not seem unduly worried by the threat to publicize details of these evictions:

Since receiving your letter, I have considered attentively the answer sent by me to the memorial of my tenantry and I can see nothing whatever to justify the expression you are pleased to make use of that it reflects upon my character or upon the prospects of my son. I do not therefore feel disposed to make any alterations in the answer I have already given to the petitioners and as far as I am concerned you are at perfect liberty to exercise whatever you may deem your duty in the House of Commons.[28]

Palmer's 'publish and be damned' reply to Moore is an insight into the mind-set of a powerful arrogant landlord who was prepared to risk the possibility of negative publicity rather than change his decision. It is ultimately a statement of his perceived right to evict when he saw fit, as well as a refusal to bow to threats.

It seems likely that the tenants who voted against McAlpine did so for religious reasons. The disenchantment of Catholics with the Tories after the Stockport riots, in tandem with the vigorous campaign run by the clergy was probably enough to convince these tenants to disregard their landlord's instructions and to support pro-Catholic candidates. Of the 15 tenants who were issued with notices to quit, four lived in the parish of Crossmolina, two in Killala, three in Moygawnagh, one each in Lackan and Kilfian whilst the remaining four tenants lived in Ballysakeery.[29] All these parishes are adjoining (see figure 12) so it is possible that some if not all these tenants colluded in their action. However, the area of these six parishes is so large that this proposition seems unlikely.

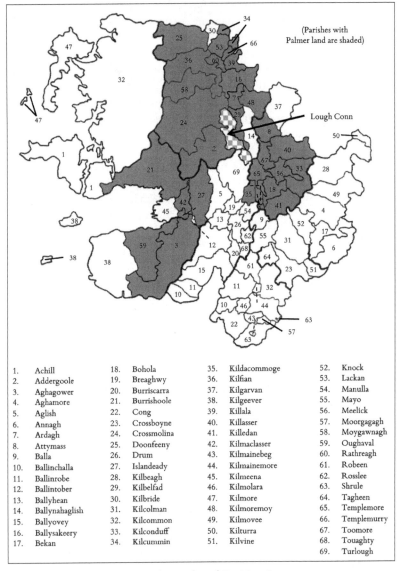

1.	Achill	18.	Bohola	35.	Kildacommoge	52.	Knock
2.	Addergoole	19.	Breaghwy	36.	Kilfian	53.	Lackan
3.	Aghagower	20.	Burriscarra	37.	Kilgarvan	54.	Manulla
4.	Aghamore	21.	Burrishoole	38.	Kilgeever	55.	Mayo
5.	Aglish	22.	Cong	39.	Killala	56.	Meelick
6.	Annagh	23.	Crossboyne	40.	Killasser	57.	Moorgagagh
7.	Ardagh	24.	Crossmolina	41.	Killedan	58.	Moygawnagh
8.	Attymass	25.	Doonfeeny	42.	Kilmaclasser	59.	Oughaval
9.	Balla	26.	Drum	43.	Kilmainebeg	60.	Rathreagh
10.	Ballinchalla	27.	Islandeady	44.	Kilmainemore	61.	Robeen
11.	Ballinrobe	28.	Kilbeagh	45.	Kilmeena	62.	Rosslee
12.	Ballintober	29.	Kilbelfad	46.	Kilmolara	63.	Shrule
13.	Ballyhean	30.	Kilbride	47.	Kilmore	64.	Tagheen
14.	Ballynahaglish	31.	Kilcolman	48.	Kilmoremoy	65.	Templemore
15.	Ballyovey	32.	Kilcommon	49.	Kilmovee	66.	Templemurry
16.	Ballysakeery	33.	Kilconduff	50.	Kilturra	67.	Toomore
17.	Bekan	34.	Kilcummin	51.	Kilvine	68.	Touaghty
						69.	Turlough

12. The parishes of Co. Mayo[30]

It is clear from the sequence of events after the 1852 election that there were estate rules for political behaviour by Lord Palmer's tenants and breaching these rules resulted in serious consequences for the tenantry. Estate rules were enforced in many other ways which the tenants had no control over. Rules regarding marriage, sharing houses, subdivision of lands and house maintenance[31] were rigidly enforced by Lord Palmer and his agents in the post-Famine period. Revd Patrick Lavelle, for instance, wrote to Lord Palmer's agent Thomas Ormsby in 1864, asking permission for his married sister to be allowed to come and live with his recently widowed mother in the townland of Mullagh which is situated in the barony of Murrisk.[32] Thomas Ormsby replied that his sister could live with her mother if she was not married, but that she would have to move out if she subsequently got married because 'the rules of the estate must be carried out'.[33] When Mrs Lavelle's daughter moved in anyway, the house was torn down and the crops were confiscated. Actions such as this by his agents enabled Lord Palmer to rigidly control many aspects of his tenants' lives.

Despite the evictions on political grounds in 1853, the rate of evictions for non-payment of rents declined sharply in the post Famine period. In 1851, 19 leasees were ejected and in 1852 a further five suffered the same fate but thereafter the number of evictions recorded in the Palmer register of leases declined to very low levels with only five evictions recorded between 1853 and 1868. The number of surrendered leases followed the same pattern with six leases surrendered in 1851, a further five in 1852 but thereafter only two leases were surrendered between 1853 and 1868.[34] These figures probably indicate that in the immediate aftermath of the Famine recovery was initially slow and that it was not until 1853 that most tenants were solvent and able to pay rents again.

Sir William Henry Roger Palmer (fourth baronet) died in 1869 and was succeeded by his son Sir Roger William Henry Palmer (fifth baronet). His period as landlord had coincided with great social, economic and demographic upheaval on his Mayo estates, bridging as it did the period of the Great Famine. He had lived a privileged existence by any standards and his everyday world was in stark contrast to the condition faced by the majority of his Mayo tenants. His failure to act positively in any meaningful way during the years of hardship caused by the failure of the potato crop, his willingness to evict tenants for non-payment of rents and his enforcement of estate rules through his agents, gained him a reputation as an uncaring, exterminating landlord, who inspired vilification rather than affection.[35]

From Palmer's perspective, the Famine period had caused him many difficulties and the fall off in rental income in combination with increasing demands for poor rates placed stringent economic demands on his finances. The 1852 electoral revolt by his tenants was viewed by him as an act of defiance and a challenge to his authority, a challenge which he met head on in order to maintain his rigid control over his Mayo tenantry.

Conclusion

The Great Famine had a greater impact on the Palmer Mayo estates than in Mayo generally. The pre-Famine social and economic structures contributed greatly to the severity of the distress. The large pre-Famine population, mainly subsistence farmers living in poor housing and on small subdivided holdings, were ill-equipped to survive a prolonged potato crop failure. When this failure occurred, many of Palmer's tenants were unable to pay rents and in consequence many were turned out from their holdings. A large but unquantifiable number of tenants died from starvation or disease or emigrated abroad.

Famine conditions prevailed into the early 1850s. Tenants from this property were evicted for non-payment of rents and also for disobeying Lord Palmer's rules and orders. The pre-Famine system of land tenure appears to have survived the Famine broadly intact on this estate, in contrast to other large Mayo properties such as that of Lord Lucan. The recovery in the agricultural sector in the mid-1850s resulted in a substantially improved economic situation for the survivors of the Famine on the Palmer estates, particularly when compared with the prevailing conditions both before and especially during the Famine.

Unlike other estates in Ireland, and in particular in Co. Mayo, Palmer did not suffer to the same extent as other landowners. He did not have to sell land in the Encumbered Estate Court, which was established in 1849 to sell properties whose owners had got into financial difficulties because their tenants had been unable to pay their rents. Between 1849 and 1857 over 3,000 properties, totalling five million acres, were disposed of by the court. It was one of the few estates able to overcome the financial problems brought about by the Famine, largely as a result of the evictions that were put in place. The tenants bore the brunt of the crisis rather than Palmer.

The political power of landowners such as Lord Palmer was not curtailed by the Famine. Throughout the 1850s, landlords behaved much as they had done in the pre-Famine period, seeking to control the political situation in counties like Mayo. Tenants were left in no doubt as to what was expected of them as large absentee landlords like Palmer issued election orders through their agents. This coercion often brought landowners into conflict with the clergy who also had power and influence over the people.

Before and after the Famine, Sir William Palmer ruled his Mayo estates with an iron grip. Tenants had to conform or suffer the ultimate consequence – that of eviction. This situation was similar to that on other properties, not only in

Mayo, but throughout Connacht. The power of landowners like Palmer only began to decline after 1870 with the introduction of the Gladstone Land act. This was the first in a series of legislative initiatives which indicated that the landlord's power was to be curbed so that he could not treat his tenants as he had before.

Notes

ABBREVIATIONS

GO   Genealogical Office
HC   House of Commons
IAA   Irish Architectural Archives
IHS   *Irish Historical Studies*
NLI   National Library of Ireland
NAI   National Archives of Ireland
RCBL   Representative Church Body Library
TCD   Trinity College Dublin

INTRODUCTION

1   Cecil Woodham-Smith, *The Great Hunger* (London, 1962).

2   Mary E. Daly, *The Famine in Ireland* (Dundalk, 1986).

3   Cormac Ó Gráda, *The Great Irish Famine* (London, 1989).

4   Christine Kinealy, *This great calamity: the Irish Famine, 1845–52* (Dublin, 1994).

5   Donald E. Jordan, *Land and popular politics in Ireland: County Mayo from the Plantation to the Land War* (Cambridge, 1994).

6   Ó Gráda, *The Great Irish Famine*, pp 59–60.

7   Canon John O'Rourke, *The Great Irish Famine* (rep. Dublin, 1974); Woodham-Smith, *The Great Hunger*; Daly, *The Famine in Ireland;* Ó Gráda, *The Great Irish Famine*.

8   James S. Donnelly, *The Great Irish Potato Famine* (Stroud, 2020); Ciarán Ó Murchadha, *The Great Famine: Ireland's agony, 1845–52* (London and New York, 2011).

9   Ciarán Ó Murchadha, *Sable wings over the land: Ennis, County Clare and its wider community during the Great Famine* (Ennis, 1998); Kathleen Villiers-Tuthill, *Patient endurance: the Great Famine in Connemara* (Dublin, 1997); Bryan MacMahon, *The Great Famine in Tralee and north Kerry* (Dublin, 2017).

10 Christine Kinealy, Jason King & Ciaran Reilly (eds), *Women and the Great Hunger* (Hamden, 2016); Christine Kinealy, Jason King & Gerard Moran (eds), *Children and the Great Hunger in Ireland* (Hamden, 2018).

11 Andrés Eiríksson & Cormac Ó Gráda, *Estate records of the Irish Famine* (Dublin, 1995), p. vii.

12 Michael Kelly, *Struggle and strife on a Mayo estate, 1833–1903: the Nolans of Logboy and their tenants* (Dublin, 2014).

13 Tom Crehan, *Marcella Gerrard's Galway estate, 1820–70* (Dublin, 2013).

14 Valuation survey of the Mayo estates of Sir W.H.R. Palmer, Bart. (NLI, MS 14075–9) (hereafter cited as Valuation survey of the Palmer estates).

15 Alphabethical register of leases belonging to the estate of Sir R.W.H. Palmer in County Mayo and Sligo (NAI, Accession 1174/2) (hereafter cited as Palmer register of leases).

16 *Returns of all notices served upon relieving officers of the poor law district in Ireland, by landowners and others, under the act of last session, 11&12 vict, intituled 'An Act for the protection and relief of destitute poor evicted from their dwellings*, HC 1849 (315), xlix, 235 (hereafter cited as *Notices served upon relieving officers of poor law districts*).

17 Donnelly, *Great Irish Potato Famine*, p. 140; see also L. Perry Curtis, *The*

depiction of evictions in Ireland, 1845–1910 (Dublin, 2011), pp 27–56.

18 The Primary Valuation of Tenements, County Mayo, 1855.

I. CONDITIONS ON THE PALMER ESTATES IN THE PRE-FAMINE PERIOD

1 Palmer papers (Valuation survey of the Palmer estates).
2 Hugh Doran Collection, IAA (17/75X4).
3 Palmer papers (Valuation survey of the Palmer estates).
4 *The census of Ireland for the year 1851, Part 1, Ulster and Connaught, area, population and housing*, HC 1852–3, [1542], xcii, 453 (hereafter cited as the *1851 Census of Ireland*). This census also contains data from the earlier 1841 Census.
5 Palmer papers (Valuation survey of the Palmer estates).
6 Brian Mitchell, *A new genealogical atlas of Ireland* (Baltimore, 1986).
7 Palmer Deeds (NAI, M6807, Box III).
8 Candidates Books and Members lists, Carlton Club, London.
9 Copy of Grant and Confirmation of Arms to Sir W.H.R. Palmer, GO MS 107, pp 206–7.
10 Palmer papers (Valuation survey of the Palmer estates).
11 Palmer register of leases.
12 Palmer register of leases. This lease was issued in 1821 for three lives at an annual rent payable of £65.
13 See for instance the lease issued to James Joyce, John Lunny, Padraig Livingstone and Hugh Geraghty dated 9 Mar. 1829, Palmer Deeds (NAI, M6807, Box II, item 350).
14 *1851 Census of Ireland*.
15 Palmer register of leases.
16 Palmer papers (Valuation survey of the Palmer estates).
17 *Returns of agricultural produce, prefatory remarks*, HC 1849 [1116] xlix, 1.
18 *Poor Inquiry (Ireland)*, supplement to Appendix (E), HC 1836[37], xxxii, 1, p. 19.
19 Ibid., p. 19.
20 Ibid., p. 23.
21 Ibid., p. 28.
22 Ibid., p. 19.
23 Barbara Kerr, 'Irish seasonal migration to Great Britain, 1800–38', *IHS* 3, no 12

(1942–3), pp 369–70; Cormac Ó Gráda, 'Seasonal migration and post-famine adjustment in the west of Ireland', *Studia Hibernica*, 13 (1973), pp 48–76.
24 *Poor Inquiry (Ireland)*, supplement to Appendix (A), HC 1835, xxvii, 1, p. 21.
25 Ibid., p. 25.
26 Ibid., p. 31.
27 Kerr, 'Irish seasonal migration to Great Britain', p. 377.
28 Ann O'Dowd, *Spalpeens and tattie hokers* (Dublin, 1991), p. 66.
29 Ibid., p. 58.
30 *Poor Inquiry (Ireland)*, supplement to Appendix (A), p. 30.
31 Ibid., p. 29.
32 *Poor Inquiry (Ireland)*, supplement to Appendix (D), HC 1836, xxxl, p. 19.
33 Kenure Park file, IAA, RW.D. 149.
34 A perspective on the moral effects of absenteeism advanced by N.D. Palmer, *The Irish Land League crisis* (New Haven, 1940), p. 30. See also Gerard Moran, 'Absentee landlordism in Mayo in the 1870s', *Cathait na Mart*, 2 (1982) pp 30–4 and Gerard Moran, *Sir Robert Gore Booth and his landed estate in Co. Sligo: land, famine, emigration and politics, 1814–1876* (Dublin, 2006).
35 Palmer, *The Irish land league crisis*, p. 33.
36 Estate papers of Palmer (NAI, Accession 1174/2/7).
37 *Report from her Majesty's Commissioners of Inquiry into the state of Law and Practice in respect of the occupation of Land in Ireland*, HC 1845 [605], xix, I (hereafter cited as the *Devon Commission*), Minutes of Evidence of George V. Jackson, p. 399 and George Irwin, p. 406, about wage levels amongst labourers in Mayo.
38 Clanmorris Mayo estate papers, 1867–68 (NLI MS 3120).
39 *Devon Commission*, Minutes of evidence of George V. Jackson, p. 396.
40 Ibid., Minutes of evidence of George V. Jackson, p. 399.
41 Ibid., Minutes of evidence of George Irwin, p. 406.
42 Ibid., Minutes of evidence of William Bland, p. 419.
43 Ibid., Minutes of evidence of Fredrick Cavendish, p. 424.
44 Ibid.
45 Ibid.

2. THE IMPACT OF THE GREAT FAMINE ON
THE PALMER MAYO ESTATES

1   Woodham-Smith, *The Great Hunger*,
p. 38.
2   Jordan, *Land and popular politics in Ireland*,
p. 71.
3   *Castlebar Telegraph*, 1 Jun. 1831.
4   *Tyrawley Herald*, 18 Sept. 1845.
5   *Tyrawley Herald*, 23 Oct. 1845.
6   'Extracts from letters addressed to the
committee, showing the condition of
the country in the winter of 1846–47',
contained in the *Transactions of the Central
Relief Committee of the Society of Friends
during the famine in Ireland in 1846 and 1847*
(Dublin, 1852), p. 185 (hereafter cited as
'Extracts of letters to the Central Relief
Committee').
7   'Extracts of letters to the Central Relief
Committee', pp 185–6.
8   *Tyrawley Herald*, 14 Jan. 1847.
9   Famine Relief Commission, incoming
letters (NAI, 2/441/44, letter number
9835).
10   Woodham-Smith, *The Great Hunger*,
p. 319.
11   *Tyrawley Herald*, 7 May 1846.
12   The surviving minute books are listed in
Deirdre Lindsey and David Fitzpatrick,
Records of the Irish Famine (Dublin, 1993),
p. 20. The minute books that do survive
are to be found in the National Library
of Ireland.
13   Famine Relief Commission, incoming
letters (NAI, 2/441/44, letter number
5804).
14   'Extracts of letters to the Central Relief
Committee', p. 89.
15   Famine Relief Commission, incoming
letters (NAI, 2/441/44, letter number
10820).
16   Famine Relief Commission, incoming
letters (NAI, 2/441/44, letter number
9835).
17   *Tyrawley Herald*, 18 Nov. 1847.
18   *Papers relating to Proceedings for the Relief
of the Distress and State of Unions and
Workhouses, sixth series, 1848*, HC 1847–8
[955], lvi, 1, p. 654.
19   Ibid., p. 665.
20   Daniel Murray Papers, File 32.4 Murray
1848, in *Archivium Hibernicum*, vol. xl,
1985, ed. Mary Purcell (hereafter cited as

Murray papers), Letter from Fr Timlin to
Fr Synnott, 26 Jan. 1848.
21   Murray papers, Letter from Fr Ward to
Fr Synnott, 4 Apr. 1848.
22   *Tyrawley Herald*, 7 Sept. 1848
23   Islandeady Parish Register (NLI,
microfilm no. p. 4212).
24   Jordan, *Land and popular politics in Ireland*,
pp 124–5. Jordan argues that the survival
of the rundale system in Mayo facilitated
early marriage.
25   Robert J. Scally, *The end of hidden Ireland:
rebellion, famine and emigration* (Oxford,
1995), p. 245, n22.
26   Murray papers, Letter from Fr Henry to
Fr Synnott, 16 Apr. 1848.
27   Islandeady Parish Register.
28   Kevin Danaher, *The year in Ireland,
Irish calendar customs* (Minnesota, 1972),
pp 39–46.
29   Islandeady Parish Register.
30   Register of the Holy Trinity Church,
Westport, Co. Mayo, parish of Aughaval,
(RCBL). Marriages are recorded only
up to 1845 so a direct comparison with
Islandeady was not possible.
31   Ibid. Details of parents' occupations are
included in the baptism register.
32   Palmer papers (Valuation survey of the
Palmer estates).
33   *1851 Census of Ireland*.
34   *1851 Census of Ireland*.
35   *1851 Census of Ireland*.
36   Palmer papers (Valuation survey of the
Palmer estates).
37   See for instance the letter to the London
Times from Revd Sidney Osborne,
16 Nov. 1849 on improvements on
the property of Lord Lucan, in Cecil
Woodham-Smith, *The reason why*
(London, 1953), pp 127–8.
38   Palmer papers (Valuation survey of the
Palmer estates).
39   Kevin Whelan, 'Settlement patterns in
the West of Ireland in the pre-famine
period' in Timothy Collins (ed.),
Decoding the landscape (Galway, 1994),
p. 69.
40   *1851 Census of Ireland*.
41   *1851 Census of Ireland*.
42   Palmer papers (Valuation survey of the
Palmer estates).
43   *1851 Census of Ireland*.
44   *1851 Census of Ireland*.

45 Palmer papers (Valuation survey of the Palmer estates).

46 *1851 Census of Ireland*.

47 Palmer papers (Valuation survey of the Palmer estates).

48 *1851 Census of Ireland*.

49 Palmer papers (Valuation survey of the Palmer estates).

50 *1851 Census of Ireland*.

51 *1851 Census of Ireland*.

52 Palmer register of leases.

53 Palmer register of leases.

54 Palmer register of leases. This register recorded alphabetically the leases issued by the Palmer estate. In the 156-year time span of the register, only 503 leases were recorded as issued, yet at times the Palmer estate population exceeded 20,000.

55 *Notices served upon relieving officers of poor law districts*.

56 *Notices served upon relieving officers of poor law districts*.

57 Woodham-Smith, *The reason why*, p. 20.

58 *1851 Census of Ireland*.

59 Mayo Outrage Papers, 1847 (NAI, 21/500).

60 Burial register of the Holy Trinity Church, Westport, Co. Mayo, parish of Aughaval (RCBL).

61 Woodham-Smith, *The reason why*, p. 118.

62 Palmer Deeds (NAI, M6807, Boxes 1–4). These boxes contain the original leases issued by the estate in Mayo. An agent for Lord Palmer in the mid-nineteenth century, Francis O'Donnell, has written in the reason for ejectment on the appropriate leases. In the period of the famine, the reason given for ejectment was exclusively for non-payment of rents.

63 Woodham-Smith, *The reason why*, pp 102, 109–10.

64 *Notices served upon relieving officers of poor law districts*. The exact numbers of persons evicted cannot be stated exactly as the returns in some cases refer to families rather than individuals.

65 Jordan, *Land and popular politics in Ireland*, pp 108–9.

66 *1851 Census of Ireland*.

67 Letter from Captain Farren to the Commissioners in *Papers relating to proceedings for the relief of the distress and state of unions and workhouses, sixth series*, 1848, HC 1847–8 [955], lvi, 1, p. 542.

3. POLITICS, EVICTIONS AND THE POST-FAMINE ECONOMIC RECOVERY ON THE PALMER ESTATES

1 Figure obtained by taking the recorded population for the Palmer estates provided by the *1851 Census of Ireland* and the *1861 Census of Ireland*.

2 *1861 Census of Ireland*.

3 Table compiled using data from *1851 Census of Ireland* and the *1861 Census of Ireland*.

4 Table compiled from data in *Returns of agricultural produce in Ireland in the year 1847, Part 1: crops*, HC, 1847–8 [923], lvii, 1, *Part 2: stock*, HC 1847–8 [1000], lvii, 1, and *Returns of agricultural produce in Ireland in the year 1856*, HC 1857–8 [2289], lvi, 1.

5 *Returns of agricultural produce in Ireland in the year 1856*, HC 1857–8 [2289], lvi, 1.

6 *Returns of agricultural produce in Ireland in the year 1847, Part 1: crops*, HC, 1847–8 [923], lvii, 1, *Part 2: stock*, HC 1847–8 [1000], lvii, 1, and *Returns of agricultural produce in Ireland in the year 1856*, HC, 1857–8 [2289], lvi, 1.

7 Rental for the estates of Sir W.H.R. Palmer in Co. Mayo and Sligo for the half year ending 1 May 1863 (NAI, Accession No. 1174/2/2).

8 The Primary Valuation of Tenements, County of Mayo, 1855.

9 The Primary Valuation of Tenements, County of Mayo, 1855.

10 *Returns of agricultural produce in Ireland in the year 1856*, HC 1857–8 [2289], lvi, 1. These returns include an appendix with statistics on emigration from Co. Mayo.

11 Palmer register of leases.

12 Clare election petition, HC 1852–3 (587), ix, 699–700, quoted in K.T. Hoppen, *Elections, politics and society in Ireland, 1832–1885* (Oxford, 1984), p. 145.

13 Hoppen, *Elections, politics and society in Ireland*, p. 145.

14 *Minutes of evidence taken before the select committee on the Mayo election petition*, HC 1852–3 (415), xvi, 221 (hereafter cited as *Select committee on the Mayo election petition* (1853)), Minutes of evidence of Francis O'Donnell, pp 29–30.

15 J.H. Whyte, *The Independent Irish Party, 1850–9* (Oxford, 1958), p. 57.

16 Ibid., p. 59.

17 *Select committee on the Mayo election petition* (1853), Minutes of evidence of Francis O'Donnell, p. 30.

18 Ibid.

19 Ibid., pp 28–9.

20 Ibid., pp 31–3.

21 Petition to Sir Roger Palmer from Patrick Gallagher and others, 1853 (Moore Papers, NLI MS 892).

22 Letter to Patrick Gallagher from Sir W.H.R. Palmer dated 14 Jan. 1853 (Moore papers, NLI MS 892).

23 Ibid.

24 Ibid.

25 Hoppen, *Elections, politics and society in Ireland*, p. 150.

26 Letter from Moore to Palmer, 23 Feb. 1853 (Moore papers, NLI MS 892).

27 Letter to Moore from Fr B. Malone, 10 Mar. 1853 (Moore papers, NLI MS 892).

28 Letter from Palmer to Moore, 28 Mar. 1853 (Moore papers, NLI MS 892).

29 Petition to Sir Roger Palmer from Patrick Gallagher and others, 1853 (Moore papers, NLI MS 892). This petition lists the names and addresses of the petitioners.

30 Developed from map in Mitchell, *A new genealogical atlas of Ireland.*

31 *Report into the working of the Landlord and Tenant (Ireland) Act, 1870 and the Acts amending same*, HC 1881, xviii, 1, Minutes of evidence of Francis O'Donnell, p. 564. O'Donnell, Palmer's agent, admitted to the Bessborough commissions that tenants were fined 5s. a piece if they did not whitewash their houses inside and out, once a year.

32 Fr Patrick Lavelle, *The Irish landlord since the Revolution* (Dublin, 1870), p. 394.

33 Ibid., p. 395.

34 Palmer register of leases.

35 See for instance Dean Burke's speech at the nomination of candidates for the 1857 Mayo elections in which he detailed exterminations practiced on the Palmer estates, reported in the *Tyrawley Herald*, 9 Apr. 1857.

Pearse Lawlor, *The outrages, 1920–1922: the IRA and the Ulster Special Constabulary in the Border campaign* (Cork, 2011).

3 Milligan, *The Walker Club*, p. 48.

4 It is notable that this incident occurred on a day already occupied by a symbolic memorial event, i.e., the anniversary of the Easter Rising. Symbolic conflict often occurs on such days, as they provide opportunities for public gatherings and media attention as well as other considerations. The Remembrance Day bombing in Enniskillen in 1987 remains the most significant example in Northern Ireland, but see below for further such coincidences in Derry.

5 *Ulster Herald*, 31 Mar. 1951.

6 Ibid.

7 Harrison, 'Four types of symbolic conflict', p. 256.

8 For more on valuation contests and Irish cultural conflict, see Máiréad Nic Craith, *Culture and identity politics in Northern Ireland* (Basingstoke, 2003), especially pp 1–24.

9 Michael Doherty, director of the Derry Peace and Reconciliation Group, interview with author, 31 July 2013.

10 Seamus Deane, *Reading in the dark* (New York, 1998), p. 130.

11 *Irish Press*, 'Troop alert for Derry', 13 July 1970.

12 Ibid. Armed guards watched the entire episode from rooftops, and riot police stood by below, but the event passed off without incident.

13 Statement of Major Hubert O'Neill at the release of the inquest findings, reported in BBC News, '1973: "Bloody Sunday" inquest accuses army', available at: http://news.bbc.co.uk/onthisday/hi/dates/stories/august/21/newsid_2500000/2500321.stm, accessed 29 July 2013.

14 Ibid.

15 *Irish Independent*, 'Now, down comes Walker after 145 years', 29 Aug. 1973; *Derry Journal*, 'Siege hero Walker felled in midnight blast', 29 Aug. 1973, reprinted 23 July 2010.

16 *Irish Independent*, 29 Aug. 1973.

17 Ibid.

18 *Derry Journal*, 29 Aug. 1973.

19 Harrison, 'Four types of symbolic conflict', p. 263.

20 Alan Day, 'Tale behind the tribute to the defender of the walls', 8 Aug. 2003, available at http://icnorthernireland.icnetwork.co.uk/features/lifestyles/page.cfm?objectid=1\3268077&method=full&siteid=91603&page=2, accessed 29 July 2013.

21 *Derry Journal*, 29 Aug. 1973.

22 *Irish Independent*, 29 Aug. 1973; Moore, interview with author, 31 July 2013.

23 On this famous Dublin structure, see Andrew O'Brien, 'The history of Nelson's pillar', *Dublin Historical Record*, 60:1 (2007), 15–23; Donal Fallon, *The pillar: the life and afterlife of the Nelson pillar* (Dublin, 2014).

24 William Moore, interview with author, 31 July 2013; *Irish Independent*, 'Apprentice Boys win £800,000', 20 Apr. 1989.

25 In recent years, until 2015, the organization operated a small museum out of the Memorial Hall and included with the £2 admission fee a 'Siege Heroes Trail' map for visitors to walk the commemorative route. See the Apprentice Boys' website for current commemorative practices, routes, and important locations: http://www.apprenticeboysofderry.org/parades.

26 BBC News, 'Apprentice Boys memorial statue attacked', 30 July 2010, available at http://www.bbc.co.uk/news/uk-northern-ireland-10817497, accessed 4 Dec. 2012.

27 Ibid. There was no official comment from Sinn Féin.

28 William Moore, interview with author, 31 July 2013; BBC News, 'Apprentice Boys of Derry £2m boost for new visitors centre', 19 Oct. 2012, available at http://www.bbc.co.uk/news/uk-northern-ireland-20001020, accessed 29 July 2013.

29 *Londonderry Sentinel*, 'Siege Museum is officially opened', available at http://www.londonderrysentinel.co.uk/news/siege-museum-is-officially-opened-1-7270867, accessed 27 Sept. 2017. Quotation from William Moore in his then capacity as chairman of the Siege Museum Management Committee.